PRAISE FOR *THE PROXIMITY PARADOX*

The Proximity Paradox is both provocative and prescriptive. It will challenge your industry experience, best practices, and team alignment. In our digital economy where creativity and innovation are in constant demand, business leaders need a new approach for meeting their client needs. *The Proximity Paradox* helps you see what you are doing wrong and how to fix it. A must-read for all agency and marketing executives.

—MK MARSDEN, THREE-TIME GLOBAL CMO,
MANAGING PARTNER AT TOUCHPOINT STRATEGIES
AND BOARD PRACTICE LEADER AT AVASTA

The Proximity Paradox isn't just a must-read for anyone in business today, it should be your manual for continually unleashing innovation in your teams and within yourself. Their approach is pragmatic, challenging, and, most importantly, hopeful.

— MATT JOHNSTON, JOHNSTON GROUP

On almost every page of this book, I found myself nodding in agreement, taking notes, or dog-earring the edge. It brings up so many points that I will now be putting in to practice in my own business. Big thank you to Kiirsten and Alex for putting this together. It's a must-read for creatives and entrepreneurs.

— PHOEBE CORNOG, CO-OWNER/FOUNDER, PANDR DESIGN CO.

I have read a ton of famous business books and *The Proximity Paradox* is one of the better ones. It's practical, relatable, and immediately applicable. I think the Proximity Paradox is a great concept, true in many ways. It gave me three ideas that I will try with my employees and a new business idea.

— STEVE ALEXANDER, OPERATIONS MANAGER, AGI WESTFIELD

I read *The Proximity Paradox* as a neuroscientist, psychologist, and business owner and from all three perspectives feel like it's great! It's like applied neuroscience without all the jargon of how the brain works. Instead it's a practical guide to taking a step back from some of the biases our brain naturally makes when we are too close or experienced in an area. I felt inspired to try these strategies with my own company and at other times affirmed with some of the strategies I already use. The examples throughout were poignant and I even caught myself laughing out loud on the streetcar. This book is a must-have for any creatives, business owners, or academics who want to stay relevant in their field for years to come.

— MANDY WINTINK, PHD, RYT, LIFE COACH, DIRECTOR,

CENTRE FOR APPLIED NEUROSCIENCE INC.

THE

PROXIMITY

PARADOX

THE
PROXIMITY
PARADOX

How to Create Distance from
Business as Usual and Do
Something Truly Innovative

ALEX VARRICCHIO *and* **KIIRSTEN MAY**

Cover design: David Drummond
Author photos: © Simeon Rusnak

LIBRARY AND ARCHIVES CANADA CATALOGUING IN PUBLICATION

Title: The Proximity Paradox : how to create distance from business as usual and do something truly innovative / Alex Varricchio and Kiirsten May.

Names: Varricchio, Alex, author. | May, Kiirsten, author.

Description: Includes bibliographical references.

Identifiers: Canadiana (print) 20190178000
Canadiana (ebook) 20190178019

ISBN 9781770415324 (softcover)
ISBN 9781773055190 (PDF)
ISBN 9781773055183 (ePUB)

Subjects: LCSH: Creative ability in business.
LCSH: Success in business.

Classification: LCC HD53 .V37 2020
DDC 658.3/14—dc23

The publication of *The Proximity Paradox* has been generously supported by the Government of Canada. *Ce livre est financé en partie par le gouvernement du Canada.* We acknowledge the support of the Government of Ontario through the Ontario Book Publishing Tax Credit, and through Ontario Creates for the marketing of this book.

PRINTED AND BOUND IN CANADA   PRINTING: FRIESENS   5 4 3 2 1

Dedicated to our families, friends, and the creative folk whose weird stories fill these pages.

CONTENTS

PREFACE

A graphic designer is invited to paint a mural on the side of an old building in a rough end of town. She collaborates with a group of artists to turn four storeys of tired brick into a contemporary work of art. When the mural is complete, the neighborhood throws a party to celebrate the first of what they hope will be many rejuvenations to the area. The graphic designer's boss reads about the mural in the news and asks her, "Why can't you create something like that around here?"

We've seen things like this happen again and again for more than ten years. As advertising agency people, we have the opportunity to work with a lot of creative types. We're not just talking about designers and artists; we're talking about people with the ability to solve old problems in new, imaginative ways. Advertising agencies and marketing departments attract thousands of these types. Yet it's rare to see a creative person unleash his or her full potential at work.

We call this effect the Proximity Paradox, and that's what this book is all about. Proximity is the effect that shackles creativity, dilutes innovation, steers brave people down safe roads, and pushes leading-edge companies to the back of the pack. It's what was blocking your view when a competitor blindsided you. It's what eventually wore down your bold, inventive younger self, and it's what is still wearing you down today.

What's paradoxical about proximity (in the literary sense of paradox) is that many of us don't view it as a hindrance. We view it as credibility and call it expertise. We set up systems to reinforce it, we teach it, and we pass it on to future generations.

The Proximity Paradox is slowly killing original thinking and, as a result, our ability to remain relevant.

We live in a world where we must innovate to survive

There has never been a more important time for people and organizations to break free from the chains of proximity. According to a report by Mark J. Perry at the American Enterprise Institute, only twelve percent of Fortune 500 firms that existed in 1955 still existed in 2016:

> It's reasonable to assume that when the Fortune 500 list is released 60 years from now in 2076, almost all of today's Fortune 500 companies will no longer exist as currently configured, having been replaced by new companies in new, emerging industries, and for that we should be extremely thankful. The constant turnover in the Fortune 500 is a positive sign of the dynamism and innovation that characterizes a vibrant consumer-oriented market economy, and that dynamic turnover is speeding up in today's hyper-competitive global economy.[1]

It's impossible for a company to adopt dynamism and innovation when the Proximity Paradox is at work. We need to restructure our teams and processes so our people can adopt the style of thinking that spurs new ideas.

It's harder than ever to win over new customers

The pressure to compete and attract customers is high. American investor Bill Gross says a product must be ten times better than the competition in order to convince a potential customer to switch. Organizations that only look to do marginally better than their competitors will never achieve the customer base they need to win.

We need to create distance from the old rival down the street and instead measure ourselves against a formidable new opponent. It's the only way we can really challenge ourselves to create the exponentially better product or service we need to acquire new customers.

The jobs of creative people are being commoditized in business

In an article she wrote for Quartz, Sarah Kessler reported that new technology allows companies to do away with hiring and just buy marketing services online. Platforms like Fiverr have dragged many creative services into the sewer of quality and price. Organizations no longer need to hire writers, designers, developers, or even advertising agencies — they can get their basic marketing work completed online for a few bucks in a few days. People who have spent years developing their craft can no longer earn a living doing great work — they must do fast work cheaply.

But people who can offer big-picture thinking, strategic services, and innovative ideas cannot be commoditized, and they will continue to find top jobs and top wages. We need to help people in commoditized industries develop these skills so that they aren't easily replaced.

Who are we to help?

We've both had the opportunity to see inside hundreds of different organizations and learn about their people, products, and businesses. We've worked with such industries as agriculture, manufacturing, construction, trade brokering, logistics, food services, real estate, law, accounting, health care, education, research, arts, and tourism, as well as with public utilities, the charitable sector, and local and regional governments.

Time and again, we've met with marketing professionals with thirty years of experience, and we've contributed ideas that they had never dreamed of. And not just within the realm of advertising, either. Our client brainstorms and discussions often stir up ideas for channel modification, new product features, and community initiatives.

Why is that? It's not us. We don't bring anything special to the table, other than our outside perspective.

We have realized that outside perspective is indeed the most valuable tool we can offer. It's more valuable than a deep knowledge of the client's business, more valuable than thirty years of marketing experience, and more valuable than the certifications required to work in their industry.

You don't have to be outside your organization to think like an outsider

A person's proximity to his or her business problem directly correlates with his or her ability to solve it. The closer you are, the harder it is to come up with the out-of-the-box ideas that are often the key to success. But when you are further away from a problem, you can see solutions that others can't.

Throughout the book, we'll look at some real-life examples of proximity. We'll share some practical tips and suggestions for you to implement, and we'll tell some first-hand stories. The stories are sometimes told by both of us and sometimes by just one of us. We haven't specified who tells each story, as it doesn't matter that much, and we thought it might be more confusing than helpful. Here's hoping that's true!

We've written this book for marketers and anyone tasked with innovation, from artists to entrepreneurs — whether it be at home, at school, or in the workplace. We look at the common places where proximity might be holding you back, and we offer exercises and thinking systems to help you create distance from a challenge so you can solve it more effectively.

INTRODUCTION

i. Recognizing the Proximity Paradox

"The experts told us to do it this way."

"Ask him; he's been here the longest."

"It's worked for us in the past; it will work again."

"We hired the most experienced person in the business."

"She started in the mailroom and now she's VP."

"That's a good idea, but they would never go for it."

"We just don't have the resources to pull that off."

"But our customers love this product the way it is."

"We might offend some people if we did that."

"This worked for our competitor, so we should do it, too."

If you've ever heard someone utter one of those statements, you're seeing the Proximity Paradox at work. It's what drives smart people to reinforce stability and predictability at the expense of creativity and innovation. And while each statement is delivered by an individual in response to a small action, over time, taken together, these statements shape the people and processes responsible for an organization's success or failure.

The Proximity Paradox is the theory that the closer you get to a challenge, the harder it is to see it for what it really is. It might seem like common sense, but it is an extremely difficult issue for businesses to manage.

Consider Kodak, the company that owned 1,100 digital imaging and processing patents. It failed to switch to digital photography, filed for Chapter 11 bankruptcy in early 2012, and sold its patents to Apple, Google, and Facebook.[2]

We can scoff at Kodak's blunder, but when we scratch the surface of the problem it faced, we realize that we are all more vulnerable than we would like to think. When you're dominating an industry, the Proximity Paradox makes it hard to see the outlier product with grainy image resolution coming to knock you down.

How can we see our own impending dangers? Statistician Nassim Nicholas Taleb wrote about this phenomenon in his book *The Black Swan*:

> Think about the secret recipe to making a killing in the restaurant business . . . The next killing in the restaurant industry needs to be an idea that is not easily conceived of by the current population of restaurateurs. It has to be at some distance from expectations. The more unexpected the success of such a venture, the smaller the *number* of competitors, and the more successful the entrepreneur who implements the idea.[3]

In business, we put a lot of stock in the current population of industry players. That's the Proximity Paradox at work again. We are close to our competitors because we benchmark our success against theirs. We set up Google Alerts on their company names, dig for clues on their product development pipeline, and challenge our own product development team to one-up them.

But if we take Taleb's example, none of the big players are going to come up with the next killer idea for their industry. When we race to perfect the film camera, we overlook the newcomer who is figuring out how to fit one on the back of a cellphone.

ii. The Birth of Proximity

While it's tempting to point blame at the people who reinforce the Proximity Paradox in our organizations, it's not their fault. Proximity isn't a choice.

Our brains are wired, and rightly so, to look for what is familiar. We are programmed to identify risk so that we can avoid it. Our schooling and training have imposed homogeneous thinking on us from the day we entered the system. As a society, we celebrate expertise and entrust the big decisions to the most tenured among us.

Human nature

People tend to crave routine — the actions we know and the experiences we can excel at. People also tend to like rituals, as they have a causal impact on our thoughts, feelings, and behaviors. Anthropologist Bronisław Malinowski suggested that people are more likely to turn to rituals when they face situations where the outcome is important, uncertain, and beyond their control.[4] That's why taking the risks needed for creativity is so fundamentally hard to do, particularly when the outcome can affect our livelihood.

Education

There is a sameness of curriculum throughout elementary school, high school, college, and university. Georgetown University's Center on Education and the Workforce recently conducted a study on education. Researchers found that workers with postsecondary education in 1973 held only twenty-eight percent of all jobs. In 2010, they held fifty-nine percent. By 2022, they are expected to hold sixty-five percent.[5] That means two-thirds of Americans will bring roughly the same education, experience, and problem-solving abilities to the workforce.

The industrial world

The comfy life we enjoy in today's post-industrialized society was built on predictability. Workers joined organizations to make their lives more predictable. These organizations operated in a predictable manner and they depended on other organizations to do the same.

In a 1995 *Harvard Business Review* article, Howard H. Stevenson and Mihnea C. Moldoveanu wrote, "What is happening to predictability in an intensely competitive, rapidly changing global economy? It is being destroyed."[6] If this was true during the year Jeff Bezos launched Amazon to the world, it is still true today.

Predictability is no longer a guarantee of success, especially in the face of disruptors capitalizing on new technology to innovate within laggard industries.

We've had the opportunity to see the Proximity Paradox work its way through the layers of human nature, education, and business in our own city. There is a popular communications program offered through a local college that attracts about fifty students per year, and it has been doing so since the 1970s. Students learn a variety of skills for jobs in the communications, media, and marketing fields. The program prides itself on instilling high standards of professionalism and a do-or-die work ethic in students.

Our city is full of program graduates to the point that alumni jokingly call themselves a mafia. Communications can be a fast-moving industry; grads don't want to risk hiring someone with a different education background who may not have the skills they themselves value.

As a result, we get similar people with similar personalities bringing the same skills and experience to the same organizations, decade after decade.

iii. Managing Proximity

I hiked the Grand Canyon for the first time in 2017. Most hikers start at the South Rim, descend the South Kaibab Trail to the Colorado River, and then hike the Bright Angel Trail back out to the South Rim. The hike out requires walking up a steep incline for seven to eight hours, and many times I had to stop to catch my breath. When I stood on the trail looking back toward the bottom, I could clearly see the zig-zagging path that I had already walked — the power of hindsight. But when I looked up ahead, I could not see the path to the top. All I could see was a narrow strip of dirt that would switchback and disappear into the rocky cliffs — the obstacles in my way. How do you get a view of the entire trail, the path to the top and a way around the obstacles? You stand on the distant North Rim and stare across the chasm.

Distance gives us the perspective we need to find our way around obstacles and reach the top. The same principle applies to innovation and coming up with imaginative new solutions to the challenges we face in business and as creative professionals.

In the chapters that follow, we'll expose the places where the Proximity Paradox is at work among people and their responsibilities, in the processes we rely on to work effectively, and in the ways we try to position ourselves for success in our industry. We'll explore why these areas are prone to the effects of the Proximity Paradox, and we'll share some strategies for how you can create the distance you need to overcome it.

Distance is not a snake oil solution — just scroll through Facebook to find the latest story of a disruptor reinventing the way we use everyday services. The chances are high that the entrepreneur behind the disruption did not come from the industry they now dominate.

For example, the founders of Airbnb did not come from the hospitality industry. Nathan Blecharczyk has a background in software engineering. Joe Gebbia is a graphic designer. Brian Chesky is an industrial designer. Similarly, the founders of Canadian company SkipTheDishes did not come from the restaurant industry. Their backgrounds were in finance, software engineering, and sales.

The two groups of entrepreneurs saw needs in the market that no company was filling: one group for couch surfing with strangers, the other for single-point-of-contact food delivery. They used the technology that was available to work out the logistics of connecting sellers and buyers. Since it was founded in 2008, Airbnb has accommodated 200 million guests.[7] SkipTheDishes was bootstrapped by the founders for three years before British company Just Eat PLC purchased it for $100 million down and another $100 million in incentives.[8]

Distance is the tried-and-true antidote to overcoming the Proximity Paradox and rekindling your relationship with your creative self.

Three fundamental steps to overcoming the Proximity Paradox

First, recognize when the Proximity Paradox is at play. We'll show you some of the top places to look in your people, your processes, and your industry.

Next, accept the fact that you may not be the best person to solve a challenge, and be OK with that. Remember, proximity isn't a choice. Feeling its effects does not reflect negatively on you or your skills and abilities. It is simply a condition of our minds and our world — a condition that you have the ability to overcome.

Lastly, create distance by shaking up the way you traditionally tackle a problem or come up with an idea. This book is full of exercises and systems you can use to do that, and we'll frame them with examples from other innovators.

PART ONE:

CREATE DISTANCE FOR PEOPLE

I am sure you can remember a time as a kid that you made a big mess. Maybe your own children have gotten carried away building an incredible fort, pulling all the toys off the shelves, or creating an entire world in which to play for hours on end. It's an important part of childhood and one that helps children exercise their imaginations. And, when you're really little, you can often get away with not cleaning it up.

I was recently talking with my sister about my three-year-old niece. She had pulled out all her toys and clothes from her room and stacked them in a large pile in the living room. It was a big pile — impressively big for a kid her age. When my sister asked what she had done, she explained that she was headed on vacation and needed to pack her toys and clothes for the journey. She then went on to explain, in great and imaginative detail, why she packed each of the toys and outfits. Some of the toys remained toys, some of the toys were her friends, and some of them served other purposes that only a three-year-old could fully understand.

The imaginary vacation took place, and when it was time to clean up, my sister ended up doing most of the heavy lifting. It's easy for a three-year-old to pull all her clothes out of the dresser, but a lot harder to fold and put them back in their rightful place.

As my niece gets older, the expectation of play will change, and as she learns how to fold her own clothes, she will ultimately become responsible for cleaning up her vacation creations. While this makes sense in a lot of different ways, it will also begin to hamper her creativity. She will only imagine and play to the extent that she is willing to clean up her mess. Her capacity to create and discover will shrink. She'll be given more and more responsibility, which will narrow the scope of what she believes is achievable.

I'm not suggesting we stop teaching kids to clean up after themselves or that we live in houses full of toys and clutter (although a lot of people with kids would attest that this happens anyway), but the analogy does raise an interesting question. If kids, or any of us for that matter, were not limited by having to deal with the outcome of what we create, could we create bigger and better things? I bet we could.

In this section, we'll look at the ways we unintentionally dampen people's creativity and let the Proximity Paradox take hold. If you own a business or manage a team, you already know that your people are your most valuable assets. But did you know they're your most valuable innovators, too? The problem is that we often ask the wrong things of them and ourselves. We need to give people the space they need to innovate.

1.

BE AN INNOVATOR, NOT AN EXECUTOR

Free yourself to think about what you could do, not what you have to do.

"Salespeople should not project manage. If a person is responsible for both the sale and management of work, then he'll only sell to the level at which he can personally manage the work. Once he reaches that threshold, he stops selling."

You've probably heard this rationale before, or something very much like it, and you can see the logic. If your project-manager salesperson sells a project, he focuses on completing it. By the time he is ready to start another project, the sales well has dried up and he has to start again from square one. It's tough to gain momentum and grow a business this way, and that's why most organizations that require both sales and project management have moved away from this approach.

Unfortunately, the old model is still common in marketing and creative-focused jobs. Instead of sales and project management being merged, it is ideation and execution. These two responsibilities are often placed on the shoulders of the same person.

Take a look at a couple of the duties we pulled from a job description for a marketing director:

The marketing director will:

- Develop and create new and forward-thinking ideas for current and possible products.
- Complete marketing department operational requirements and be responsible for the execution of department projects.

It's a common job description, but in reality, balancing these two expectations can quickly become an almost impossible task. And without both product development and project management, the employees and organization will suffer.

What's the alternative? You could make the case to totally separate these responsibilities into two different roles, arguing that you need a B-type right-brainer to develop the forward-thinking ideas and an A-type left-brainer to excel at their execution. But the reality for most professionals is that their jobs are not going to change. Most organizations cannot afford to hire a second senior marketer to take on half of the marketing director's role, and your CFO will tell you that every job is going to require elements of creativity and elements of execution.

Instead, we need to learn to manage these conflicting responsibilities within ourselves.

Where have you built your ceiling?

Each of us has our own innovation ceiling and execution ceiling. Our innovation ceiling represents the extent to which we can think creatively. It's the highest reaches of our imagination and creative potential. It's pretty damn high.

Our execution ceiling is much lower. It represents our threshold for delivery, our ability to take an idea, deliver it, and make it real and tangible. The execution ceiling height is determined by our skill set, timelines, budget, competing responsibilities, and physical and emotional energy. These are the challenges to which we are in close proximity.

Until you can separate innovation and execution within yourself, you will only innovate to the level at which you can execute the idea. To be effective, we need to create distance between our innovation brain and our execution brain.

Fig. 1: The difference between innovation and execution ceilings.

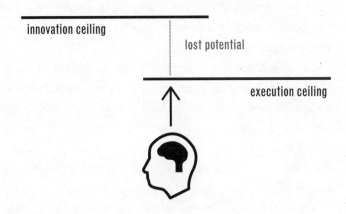

Different ceilings can create tension between teams

Conflict can arise when two people are working with different ceilings. I experienced it firsthand in my early days working as the creative director of an advertising agency.

There were two people involved in a working relationship: my agency's junior account manager and the director of marketing for one of our clients. I saw there was a tension between them and wondered where it was coming from.

I was joining the junior account manager (essentially a junior marketer) at a client meeting. In the car on the ride over, she briefed me on where things were at. We had recently presented the client with an annual marketing plan and were going in to review feedback.

On our drive, I got the sense that the junior account manager was frustrated with the client. She talked a lot about what she had put into the plan, why it was so great, and how it was going to move the needle. She couldn't understand why the client was pushing back on it. She spoke about the client in a patronizing manner, saying things like, "He just doesn't get it" and "I'll have to explain it to him in person."

When we arrived at our meeting, we sat down with the client. My role was essentially to watch and listen — see how things were going and assess whether the client was getting what we had promised them.

I had felt strange about the interaction in the car, as the conversation wasn't a new one for me. Agency people will often say, "The client doesn't get it" or "The client doesn't know what's best for their brand." It's easy to shrug these comments off and attribute them to agency egos.

But something about this particular meeting cemented things for me. Here we were, in the client's boardroom, and a junior account manager fresh out of school was slowly explaining the basics of marketing to a director with twenty-five years' experience like it was the first time he'd heard about the Four Ps. The level of condescension shocked me. The longer the junior account manager explained the intricacies of a direct mail campaign, the more the seasoned marketer dug in his heels.

What we were all missing at the table was that our account manager was wearing her innovation hat and the client was wearing his execution hat. We weren't having a conversation about the same thing, so of course we weren't connecting.

The tension and miscommunication were perpetuated by the differences between the parties' innovation and execution ceilings. The junior account manager had a high innovation ceiling — she was new to the role and full of excitement and ambition.

The marketing director's innovation ceiling was also, no doubt, very high. But in that particular meeting, his execution ceiling was getting in the way.

His existing team had to complete all the work with the existing marketing budget. They were understaffed, and our recommendations would require changing some of their systems, which would have put more work on the already stretched team. The fixed budget meant he couldn't hire other professionals to complete the work. The marketing director couldn't see the value in the recommendations — he could only see bad ideas.

We failed to recognize the factors that were making the client's execution ceiling lower than our agency's innovation ceiling. Instead, each party assumed the other was being ignorant.

The ceiling affects anyone tasked with bringing an idea to life

I continued to see this trend of condescension from agency people for years to come, coupled with their belief that in-house marketers don't "get it" or don't know what's best for their organizations. I constantly had to remind people that agency marketers and in-house marketers all have the same education and training, and we all have the same passion for creative ideas. We just happen to work on different sides of the fence.

I have been on the opposite side of the fence from in-house marketers for most of my career. I would come into their organizations and present out-there ideas that could push their brands in new and different directions. I feel confident doing this; it's a skill that comes naturally to me.

For a few years, though, I switched sides of the fence and became my agency's director of marketing. My sole focus was promoting our agency and bringing in new clients. All of a sudden, my creativity dropped, my ideas turned safe, and I took what should have been a very exciting job and made it vanilla. From the outside, I could have suggested dozens of amazing initiatives to market our agency. But from the inside, it was much more difficult because I had to both develop and execute the initiatives.

This experience showed me that both in-house and agency marketers are fully capable of ideation and innovation, but the in-house marketer is handicapped by his or her proximity to the challenge and the limitations they see in the organization and the brand.

For example, if I asked you to brainstorm new ways of selling cars (assuming you don't currently sell cars), I bet you could come up with a laundry list of cool ideas. This is because your innovation ceiling is high and your execution ceiling doesn't exist. Try doing the same for your industry. I bet it's a lot harder.

Your proximity to the challenge determines the height of the ceiling

Each of us has both an innovation ceiling and an execution ceiling that directly affects our ability to develop ideas.

For the agency marketers, execution isn't as much of a concern. In fact, creative directors and senior creative talent couldn't be more distant from that responsibility. They are busy dreaming up bold, never-before-seen ideas that would make people think differently about the client's brand. They are measured on their ability to come up with novel, innovative, and out-there ideas.

For in-house marketers, or even agency people who manage the client's day-to-day marketing, it's a different story. They have both innovation and execution responsibilities, so their ideas will match what they believe they can reasonably and practically execute. Members of this group are measured on their ability to set their organizations up for success. When you pursue novel, innovative, and out-there ideas, there's a real chance you will fail.

When there are no strings attached to ideas, we can dream big. When we have finite resources to make the dream happen, we rein in the ideas accordingly. This is the Proximity Paradox at work. Your rational brain stymies your creative brain by dredging up all the challenges close at hand: the resources you have available on your team, the budget constraints, the looming due date, the strict brand standards, the even more strict legal department, the stakeholders, the shareholders, and the fact that your name will be attached to this project for the rest of time.

How do you divide responsibilities?

Whether it's my niece creating an imaginary world out of clothes or a marketer innovating for his or her brand, we all inevitably complete the task in one of two ways:

1. We only make the mess. We do the creating and ideating, and someone else cleans it up.
2. We do it all. The creation, ideation, and cleanup all fall on our shoulders.

The first scenario is the pipe dream. It's why very small children can commit so fully to play, and it's why some of the best inventors don't ever try to commercialize their work. They create, imagine, and mess things up, and then someone else comes in to deal with the outcome or end product.

The rest of us have to wear many hats. The secret to success is recognizing when the Proximity Paradox is steering your thinking, and then donning the hat you need for the task at hand.

How Skunk Works Teams
compare to Innovation Colonies

Let's look at two different approaches to innovation and execution within an organization: Skunk Works teams and Innovation Colonies. In a Skunk Works model, the team is given autonomy and freedom to come up with a product idea and then build it. In an Innovation Colony, the team focuses on innovation alone. Where do these models come from, and what are they capable of producing? We're glad you asked.

Skunk Works and the race to build a hydrogen-fueled engine

Skunk Works was the name first given to describe a top-secret program run by aerospace and defense company Lockheed Martin. The goal was to design and build a new jet fighter aircraft prototype during the Second World War. It needed to fly at speeds up to 200 miles per hour faster than the company's existing jet fighter model at the time, but the US government gave the company a deadline of just 180 days to develop it.

The initial problem facing Lockheed Martin was that its manufacturing plant floor space was fully occupied with building its existing model to cope with the demands of the war. The only option was for the new model's design engineers and mechanics to set up their operations in a rented circus tent away from the main plant. That tent was next to a plastics factory that emitted foul smells, and the Skunk Works moniker evolved to describe the operation.

The Lockheed Martin team developed its new jet fighter in just 143 days, well ahead of schedule. The success encouraged the company to continue this separate approach for the design and development of its new innovations. The company even trademarked the Skunk Works name.

The Skunk Works approach can have limitations, however. Consider a later, less successful experience of Lockheed Martin's Skunk Works operation.

By 1956, Lockheed Martin and the US government were looking to innovate further. They wanted to develop a spy plane that was powered by liquid hydrogen. They therefore needed to build a hydrogen-fueled engine. The top-secret project involving the CIA and Lockheed Martin was named Suntan and the organization promised to have a prototype ready within 18 months.

There were no known applications of liquid hydrogen at the time. It is a highly flammable substance, so there were legitimate safety concerns about how it could be effectively stored and used to fuel an aircraft. It requires special refrigeration and expert handling.

Because of its earlier success, Lockheed Martin's Skunk Works team began work on the Suntan project. However, they had some competition. The Cold War that began after the Second World War was in full swing in the 1950s. A brilliant Russian scientist whom Stalin had imprisoned for refusing to work on an atomic bomb had been released, and he was an expert on liquid hydrogen. He, too, began working with a team in Russia to develop the world's first hydrogen-fueled engine.

While attempting to build their prototype, it became apparent to the Skunk Works team members that the plane would only have the capacity to fly for 2,000 miles without refueling. To reach Russia for its intended use as a spy plane, it would need to regularly refuel at strategically placed land bases in Europe and Asia. These bases would need the ability to safely store the highly flammable liquid hydrogen.

The logistics of organizing this were extremely costly and problematic, especially for a highly secretive operation like a jet fighter. Leaders of the Suntan project eventually met with the Pentagon in mid-1957 and advised that the project be officially cancelled, which it was not long afterward.

However, within months of the cancellation, the Russians successfully launched the world's first hydrogen-fueled satellite (Sputnik 1) into orbit. Sputnik 1 completed 1,440 orbits of the globe in twenty-one days, before safely burning up when it inevitably ran out of fuel and re-entered Earth's atmosphere.

This innovation demonstrated the Soviet Union's technological capacity and its ability to gather military intelligence information. The development triggered the "space race" as the next frontier in the Cold War, with both the Soviet Union and the US ramping up their spaceflight and satellite navigation development efforts.

Why did the Russian liquid hydrogen engine project succeed while Suntan failed?

You could argue that Lockheed Martin's Skunk Works approach saddled it with execution concerns, as opposed to having complete freedom to explore and develop innovative ideas for the potential use of a liquid hydrogen-fueled engine. These execution concerns potentially limited the team's creative thinking.

The members of the Skunk Works team were more concerned with the execution logistics of refueling a spy airplane on Earth. Unlike the Russians, they failed to see the potential for an alternative liquid hydrogen-powered satellite that could be built for a similar military intelligence purpose.

This example demonstrates how creativity can be inhibited by the inherent nature of the execution ceiling, in this case the one that exists within the Skunk Works approach. The execution ceiling can prevent an organization from reaching its innovation potential and subsequently developing a successful new product.

The Skunk Works term has evolved to describe any general business approach for separating small innovation teams away from the rest of an organization, enabling them to work more flexibly, independently, and confidentially. This approach became a very popular method for organizations looking to develop innovations in the second half of the 20th century.

In many ways, Skunk Works teams operate like modern-day start-up companies. They are responsible for both innovation and execution. However, smaller start-ups have some advantages over medium- and larger-sized organizations (including those that have Skunk Works teams operating) when it comes to disrupting markets with their innovations.

Smaller start-ups aren't constrained by needing to execute with their existing products and services like larger established organizations are. They can focus on disruption and aggressively chase market share, rather than having to also worry about defending their entrenched market position.

In today's highly competitive business environment, disruption is both a constant threat and an opportunity. In the 20th century, organizations could largely survive by making incremental improvements to their products and services. Now they are more vulnerable than ever to disruptive innovations, particularly those brought on by technology. There are numerous examples of companies that have fallen victim to disruptive innovation: Kodak, Blockbuster, and BlackBerry, just to name a few.

To survive and thrive, 21st-century organizations need to develop a culture of continuous, disruptive innovation and improvement. This is a major change in thinking from 20th-century business practices, where these activities tended to be controlled and executed by separate organizational entities like Skunk Works.

To disrupt like a start-up, you need to maximize your organization's creativity and innovation potential. That potential can't be constrained by your execution ceiling. That's where an Innovation Colony approach is likely to deliver better results, because it is solely focused on innovation.

Innovation Colonies do it better

Innovation Colony is a term coined by software, consultancy, and educational entrepreneurs Trevor Owens and Obie Fernandez in their 2014 book, *The Lean Enterprise: How Corporations Can Innovate Like Startups*. Innovation Colonies work as autonomous entities within an organization, rather than operating separately from it.[9]

There are other key differences between Innovation Colonies and Skunk Works:

1. An Innovation Colony is responsible solely for developing innovations, not for their execution as well (as Skunk Work teams are). This encourages boundaries to be pushed, rather than be limited by execution constraints. It enables larger, more disruptive ideas to be developed and nurtured.

2. Members recruited for the Innovation Colony should be the most creative, independent, and driven people in the organization, not necessarily the smartest or most pragmatic people (who may be more suited to execution roles). Having the right people in the Innovation Colony helps raise the organization's innovation ceiling potential.

3. The activities of the Innovation Colony aren't secretive. Collaboration and openness with the rest of the organization is encouraged. Indeed, it is necessary so that the innovation and execution functions work productively together to carry out their respective roles. This also helps the innovation culture to become part of the organization's DNA.

4. The members of the Innovation Colony typically give up a portion of their salary in exchange for equity

in the ideas they are developing. This encourages an entrepreneurial spirit. It recognizes the fact that many of the most successful disruptive innovations in recent times have been developed by start-ups (who obviously have equity in the ideas that they develop).

In a sense, the equity helps the Innovation Colony members become motivated "intrapreneurs" for the larger organization. From the organization's point of view, that's better than the potential alternative: that their talented, creative people become frustrated by the bureaucracy that often exists in larger organizations and leave to start their own ventures. In those situations, they become external entrepreneurs and competitors. Their creative, disruptive ideas could potentially threaten the future success of the organization they left.

There are several recent examples of this happening, even in a seemingly innovation-friendly environment, such as Google. The company is famous for encouraging innovation through initiatives like "twenty percent time" (where designated staff can spend twenty percent of their time working on developing their own projects, which could potentially benefit Google). This initiative has led to Google News, Gmail, and AdSense.[10]

However, the Google staff who developed these ideas didn't have any direct equity in their future success. The company has had plenty of creative people leave and take very successful ideas with them to launch their own start-up ventures over the years. High-profile examples include Ev Williams (Twitter), Kevin Systrom (Instagram), and Dennis Crowley (Foursquare).[11]

It would have been better for Google if these people had been more motivated to stay at the company to exploit these disruptive ideas. They each obviously had very high innovation ceilings, and an Innovation Colony approach could have ensured that this wasn't inhibited in any way. That's because the execution function is separate from ideation in the Colony approach.

While the Innovation Colony is a relatively new approach, and it's still early days in terms of its implementation and results, companies that are trying it include such noted innovators as Adobe and Disney.[12]

Strategies for creating distance from your responsibilities

Most of the people reading this book will have active execution ceilings as well as active innovation ceilings. You've likely got someone outside your office door telling you that you need to be more creative, that you've got to do more to move the needle and innovate.

In addition, you've probably got someone else (or the same person, which is even more irritating) reminding you to watch your budget, keep staff numbers down, and mind the conservative board members when you are coming up with new ideas. Hello rock and hard place, nice to meet you.

So what do you do? How do you free yourself from the Proximity Paradox and create the distance you need to reach for your innovation ceiling? Well, you can start by closing your office door (if you are lucky enough to have one). Then you can break the problem down into smaller stages so you might have a semblance of hope in trying to solve it. Because let's face it, it's not easy. And we're not all going to be able to institute Skunk Works teams or Innovation Colonies in our workplaces.

Here are a few ways to separate execution from innovation within your own mind. You'll feel more in control of the outcome, and you might even get better at wearing each hat.

Acknowledge your limitations

The first step in letting your brain change and adapt to two conflicting realities is acknowledging that they exist. This might sound really simple, but unfortunately it's not. Countless marketers with whom I speak beat themselves up over this — they feel like they are idea killers when they really are quite passionate about good ideas.

They resent the agencies with which they work because they are constantly told "No" and "That won't work because . . . " They also feel as though they are failing as marketers because they can't juggle innovation and execution while still feeling creatively fulfilled and getting work out the door efficiently.

If this is you, you are not a bad marketer, you are not an idea killer, and you're more than capable of coming up with game-changing work that will give your company the ROI it's after. You can be the person to spearhead creative and marketing evolution in your organization and get everyone else to see the light.

Start practicing this habit: At the outset of a conversation, brainstorm, or meeting, ask the group whether you are having an innovation/creation conversation or an execution/delivery conversation. Share your own expectations with the group. As much as you can, try to separate these two lines of thinking.

To take it one step further, schedule two thirty-minute meetings and devote one to innovation and one to execution. You'll be more effective in two short, focused meetings than one hour-long meeting where you bounce back and forth between the ceilings.

Hold a disruptor brainstorm

Once you've acknowledged that you are not useless and that your current marketing predicaments are more a symptom of your proximity to the challenge than they are an indication of your own potential, it's time to try a few things to create some distance between your execution and innovation ceilings.

Try a disruptor brainstorm. If you think about disruptors, they rarely come from inside the industry. They have little to no marketing experience and brainstorm from very different perspectives. In this exercise, you want to think like a disruptor. Ignore the execution constraints you've wrestled with, dial back your industry knowledge, look at your company at a surface level, and think about the game in a different way. In other words, step back and look at your business not from the perspective of a marketer who works in it, but instead as an outsider from an entirely different space.

Set aside two hours (even better if it's three) and gather your team, ideally in an off-site location. You are going to spend time together brainstorming ways to improve a company just like yours. For the sake of this exercise, it's better to choose a different name so that you don't bring the same constraints to the table. If your company is called ACME, change it to BACME for the sake of the exercise.

There are three "what would it look like" scenarios below. Spend thirty-five minutes blue-sky thinking on each of them. Be willing to challenge your current assumptions, and try to imagine a totally different world in which your hypothetical company exists.

The goal here is not to develop concrete ideas that you can execute tomorrow, but to free your mind and explore the reaches of your innovation ceiling.

What would our company look like if:

1. We got rid of marketing altogether and had to rely on other methods to grow our business?
2. We marketed and structured ourselves like a totally different industry? (For example, if you are a B2B, explore a B2C model and vice versa. Choose an industry

before you start brainstorming, and do a bit of research to gain a high-level understanding of how it operates, its markets, operating budgets, etc.)

3. Our marketing budget tripled in size tomorrow and the nay-sayers in the company all said, "Yes"?

It's not easy to break up your traditional lines of thinking, and it's not always going to feel productive. When you enter the disruptor brainstorm, leave your issues at the door. Take this exercise seriously, keep the group on task, and make sure it doesn't turn into three hours of airing grievances.

Once you have completed your brainstorm, go through each of the ideas that you've come up with and talk about why you would (or wouldn't) be able to execute them. Look closely at recurring constraints and see if you can generate ideas on how to eliminate them. You may also want to share this ideas list and accompanying constraints with the rest of your senior management team. It can elevate the appetite for innovation in your company.

Lastly, try choosing one of the more out-there ideas and putting together a plan to champion it through your organization. One victory can often create the company buy-in you need to pursue more innovative ideas.

Separate concept and execution teams

On an upcoming project, try separating your team into two groups: a concept team and an execution team. The first group will be responsible for creating the idea or concept for the project. The second group will bring that concept to life. Keep the teams separate until the concept team has solidified its idea, otherwise the execution team might raise flags that limit the freedom of thought.

Get the concept team to develop an idea that excites the team members, has few limits and boundaries, and fulfills the project objectives. Make them present the concept to you, and then present it to the execution team together. Work with the executors to develop a plan to build and launch the campaign, product, or initiative. Recognize that some elements of the concept may have to change, but challenge the execution team to do its very best to make it work.

For the next project, switch up the teams. Changing responsibilities will keep everyone motivated and fresh. The simple separation of the idea creation and execution functions can help your people recognize their proximity to challenges, give them a chance to create some distance from them, invite more creative thinking within your organization, and significantly improve the quality of your output.

2.

LISTEN TO THE
NEW BLOOD

Tenured staff are limited by hindsight,
so look to new people to get new ideas.

When you're looking for new answers to new
questions, it is knowledge itself that blocks progress. It is knowledge that creates real ignorance,
just as wealth creates poverty. Every time a new
discovery is made, enormous new areas of ignorance are opened up.[13]
— Marshall McLuhan (1970)

Seniority and responsibility often correlate in the workplace, government, and academia. But did you know seniority and problem-solving
ability are also closely related? Years of experience come with both
wisdom and limitations.

As people become more senior in their careers or their fields,
they are entrusted with more and more innovation responsibilities.
It is often up to those with the most experience to solve the biggest problems. But a person's years of experience do not necessarily
make her the most creative. If that person is used to doing things

a certain way and sees no need to change a formula, she isn't likely to do it.

The restriction on creativity here is our proximity to our own experience. The more you know about a subject or organization, the more your thinking can be constrained.

For example, it took an intern working at Shreddies to come up with a creative campaign that revived the brand in a way that no one more senior could have imagined. It took a group of kids brainstorming ideas on water conservation to develop an entirely new sidewalk system for the city of Amsterdam; one that so impressed civil engineers they decided to start prototyping.

Whose input do you value most?

For many years, career advancement in organizations would look like this: start in the mailroom, prove your gumption to the higher-ups, get promoted to assistant, then manager, then director, and finally CEO. Companies celebrate these kind of success stories, and, as a society, we admire them. Everyone loves an underdog whose hard work pays off.

The underdog learns every side of the business on his climb to the top. He becomes the most knowledgeable and experienced team member, and that gives him a lot of influence. Other staff members look to him for mentorship, new ideas, and guidance. When we are faced with a crucial decision or major roadblock, we seek his counsel. When deciding the direction the company should take, we don't move until we get his input.

We value the wisdom of underdogs-turned-leaders. They know the people who have come and gone, the ins and outs of the company, and the products, promotions, and projects that worked ten years ago, seven years ago, and within the last eighteen months. We trust their knowledge of the past to solve our challenges of the future.

You may not have a former underdog on your company's leadership team, but you certainly have senior leaders who play the same role within your organization. They steer the organizational ship to the destination that they think offers the best shake for shareholders, staff, and customers. They often define the appetite for risk within a company.

When presented with a new idea or emerging trend, a senior person in a company can be the first to say, "We tried that three years ago and it flopped" or "The CEO will never go for it because our competitors tried it and failed," or "That's too much risk; we'll get mud on our face." These senior staff might instead focus on one approach that has worked for them for the last five years. Their proximity to their companies' past failures keeps them looking in one direction for solutions. They may not be able to look beyond their organizations to consider the small ways the customers or business environment has changed. What once might have seemed ludicrous is now a viable option.

Every year of employment puts more constraints on problem-solving ability

People who are very senior in a company can have too narrow a view to solve problems effectively. They can be too close to the work — and to their tried-and-tested ways — to see the big picture or consider tackling a problem from a different angle. Staying within a certain proximity to what's worked in the past minimizes risk and protects the company's money and reputation. It also protects the senior staff members' jobs.

While it makes sense from a stability standpoint to stick to the tried-and-tested approach, it can stall the company's growth. Leaders know that companies need to evolve to stay relevant, particularly in this era where dynamic start-ups are giving long-established businesses a run for their money. Until we take a step back and accept a certain amount of risk, we'll never see the alternative routes to grow and evolve.

One amazing example of this paradox at work is the forty-five-degree turn that Post Foods Canada Corporation made with one of its brands.

The dazzling success of Diamond Shreddies

Shreddies is a wheat breakfast cereal currently manufactured by Post Foods Canada Corporation. Other cereal brands in its product range include Sugar Crisp, Grape Nuts, Raisin Bran, and Shredded Wheat. Shreddies was first produced in 1939 and is available in Canada, New Zealand, and Great Britain.

One of the company's most successful product marketing ideas in recent years was developed by a twenty-six-year-old intern at Ogilvy, Post Foods's advertising company. To use a pun, it was an "out of the box" idea centered on the shape of each individual Shreddie inside each cereal box.

The breakfast cereal market is intensely competitive, with large multinational companies like Kellogg's and General Mills[14] prepared to spend millions of dollars on their products and associated marketing campaigns.

After nearly seventy years in the market, Shreddies sales had been mature and declining two percent year-on-year for the previous decade.[15] One thing that breakfast cereal manufacturers generally do over time to increase sales is to change their products in some way. But people weren't dissatisfied with the Shreddies product. In fact, market research indicated that existing users didn't want Shreddies to change. Many Canadian parents had grown up with it, even though their kids weren't enthused by it.

That presented a challenge. How do you increase the sales of a well-known product when existing buyers don't want it to change, and new generations aren't enticed by it anymore?

That was the question Shreddies presented to Ogilvy. Their brief was simple: get consumers talking about Shreddies again, without changing the product. The Shreddies team wanted a proposal for an innovative advertising campaign. Prior to that, there had been no significant marketing investment in the Shreddies brand for fifteen years.[16]

Each Shreddie in its cereal box has a square shape. They always have (and probably always will). However, when advertising intern named Hunter Somerville was tasked with coming up with an idea for the back of the Shreddies cereal box, he set out to make people laugh. His idea for an "old" square Shreddie versus "new" diamond-shaped Shreddie challenge was unveiled to the senior Ogilvy team, and people laughed out loud.[17]

It was intended as a joke. But Ogilvy's creative director Nancy Vonk saw a spark in the idea. She could see the problem that Shreddies had, and thought this might just be quirky enough to fix it somehow. "Canadians like Shreddies, but they had forgotten all about them," she recalled. "Our goal was to do whatever it takes to make people think about them again."[18]

She asked Somerville to think about it some more and write it up as a potential campaign proposal. He subsequently did, fleshing the idea out to the point where he no longer thought it was just a silly joke. He envisioned consumers having to make a choice: buy the old traditional square Shreddies that they know and love, or try the "new" diamond version. That would get them thinking about the brand and engaging with it, something Shreddies consumers (and others) hadn't done for a long time.

They subsequently presented the campaign proposal to Post Foods Canada Corporation, and the organization loved it!

The Shreddies product itself didn't need to change at all for the campaign to be successful; it was simply about how people perceived the product. That would hopefully lead to increased sales. Post Foods even produced a special "mixed" pack of square and diamond-shaped Shreddies for consumers who were undecided, even though they were the same product!

The advertising campaign further encouraged the illusion with the catchphrase, "The same 100 percent whole-grain wheat in a delicious diamond shape."[19] It made tongue-in-cheek claims that the world's leading designers had come up with the new shape and that it was forty-five percent more delicious.

A multimedia promotional campaign was developed featuring television, print, and web advertising, as well as outdoor billboards, viral videos, a website, and a package redesign. All the elements of the promotional campaign featured a prominent diamond Shreddie. The theme was that the old square-shaped Shreddies were boring and that the new diamond-shaped Shreddies were exciting. The subtheme was that Shreddies are already as good as they can get, and they always have been.

The TV ads were set up to look like hidden-camera focus groups. The actors in the ads were asked to compare both the look and the taste of the square and diamond-shaped Shreddies, and to rate their preferences. The actors naturally gave the diamond shape the tick of approval, indicating that it both tasted better and looked more interesting. The ads concluded by encouraging consumers to compare the square and diamond shapes, too (to encourage Shreddies sales as well as awareness of the "new" variety). They could then go to diamondshreddies.com to vote for their preference.

Within twenty-four hours of the launch of the campaign, it had gone viral. Consumers generally liked the joke and ran with it. Most (hopefully) understood quickly that the product hadn't changed at all, but liked the unusual idea. But others were less certain whether Diamond Shreddies was a new product or not. There were debates on online forums and social media. The company even received a letter from an apparently concerned consumer, which read:

> I'd like to know how much money your firm actu-
> ally paid someone to produce Diamond Shreddies?
> A square on its side? How stupid can you be?

The company maintained the spirit of its campaign in its formal response to the letter-writer, allegedly written by the "President of Shreddies":

> Thanks for your question. We don't disclose our
> advertising budgets, but let me assure you that a
> square on its side is still merely a square.[20]

Within two months of the campaign's launch, the Diamond Shreddies website had attracted more than 95,000 unique visitors. Fifty-five Facebook Groups had also been created.[21] People were even taking photographs of the billboards, recalled creative director Nancy Vonk.[22]

Forecast sales for the campaign doubled, with the company selling out of four months' worth of "limited edition" Diamond Shreddies stock within two months. Overall sales of Shreddies increased by eighteen percent.[23]

For the record, the online preference votes during the campaign finished at sixty-two percent for Diamond Shreddies versus thirty-eight percent for the original square version. And even if people didn't participate in voting or think that the joke was that funny, they still noticed the ad and the Shreddies product. The campaign also generated hundreds of stories in both print and digital media, including being the cover story on several prominent business and marketing magazines. That sort of free publicity for a product is gold.

The Diamond Shreddies campaign revived interest in the Shreddies brand without the product needing to change at all. Post Foods Canada Corporation enjoyed the benefit of a product line extension without actually creating one!

The advertising campaign was fun, smart, and memorable, winning a prestigious international Clio Award for advertising in 2008.[24] The campaign also won a Grand Prix CASSIES award, which acknowledges the ability of an advertising campaign to generate client business.[25]

Advertising guru Rory Sutherland paid tribute to the campaign:

> This is the most perfect case of creating intangible, added value, without changing the product in the slightest. How many problems of life can actually be solved by tinkering with perception, rather than that tedious, hardworking, and messy business of actually trying to change reality?

The success of the campaign also helped launch Somerville's career. He didn't stay an intern for long. He was hired soon after as a full-time copywriter, and after spending two-and-a-half years at Ogilvy, he has since worked both as a staff member and freelancer for other major advertising agencies, including DDB and Saatchi & Saatchi. He has been ranked among the top five creatives in the advertising industry in both Canada and the UK.[26]

Good ideas can come from anywhere in an organization, not necessarily from the most experienced or senior people. For a company to develop a culture of innovation, we need to encourage all potential idea sources to contribute.

We need to look at problems from different angles to generate creative solutions (literally in this case for Diamond Shreddies, but the general principle is valid for any problem).

Young people can come up with very creative ideas. If leaders at Ogilvy hadn't taken an intern's idea for Diamond Shreddies seriously, they never would have developed what became an award-winning and successful campaign for their client.

Idea champions are important. If Ogilvy's creative director hadn't seen the potential in her intern's idea, it most likely never would have seen the light of day. Seemingly silly ideas can be very creative and generate marketing results that expensive product upgrades or modifications can't necessarily deliver. The Diamond Shreddies case provides ample evidence.

Your own experience and expertise can often work against you

We often think that our most senior people are the most capable of coming up with our best solutions or that increasing a person's responsibility will increase their positive influence on the organization.

Unfortunately, as responsibility increases, risk tolerance decreases. And with every year of work and every letter you add to the end of your name, you develop a deeper and more focused understanding of the world you live in, making it harder to see what might be happening outside.

To be successful, we need to create distance from our own expertise and distance from the responsibilities, the expectations and the structure of the workers in our companies. As long as you're focused on what you still have to achieve, you won't be able to accomplish what you're capable of achieving.

Strategies for creating distance from your own experience

While you can't shut off your proximity to your own experience, you can create an environment that encourages the new blood to contribute ideas. We're not just talking about young staff; anyone from a different department or background or a new employee who came from a different organization or industry will look at your company's problems in a way you never can.

Be prepared to accept change

Tenured staff may not see any reason to invest more time and money in the marketing budget or to come up with new ideas when the old ones work just fine. Hone your change management skills to help others be open and receptive to new ideas. If the culture isn't fully on board with a new person making changes, the changes won't stick, and the person won't stick around. Before long, the company will resume its old ways.

Matchmake within your organization

Pick the next project or problem to solve, and instead of putting it on the desk of an expert, create a tag team. If you're considered the expert in that project, recognize that you won't be able to innovate freely, and then find someone who can. Recruit a teammate — someone with whom you wouldn't typically work — and combine his or her fresh ideas with your insight to develop some alternatives to your normal course of action.

When pairing up experts and innovators, consider your entire team, regardless of their roles or their seniority within your company. While it might not typically make sense within the company culture to have a junior designer working as an innovator with a senior production manager, when the goal is creativity, it can bring new ideas and energy to a project.

The combination of different staff members can also speed up the implementation of an idea. We've all worked on projects that are great in theory but fall flat because they weren't executed properly. Assigning an innovator to an expert relieves the pressure on the expert to do everything himself or herself, or of shouldering all the responsibility when things don't go to plan.

Assign roles in team brainstorms

When you host a team brainstorm, are there a few big personalities who steer the discussion? Do participants defer to the most senior person in the room? Do some people sit on their hands while others draw on the walls?

People have certain brainstorm styles, and when they consistently revert to the same old styles, it can create a group dynamic that limits diversity of thought. To combat this problem, try assigning roles to participants.

The Flag Bearer

This person is often the owner of the challenge. He can clearly define the problem and take others on a journey to solve it, painting a picture of where we've come from and the grand potential of where we might be able to end up. The Flag Bearer inspires others to take action. He brings the most value through his passion, not necessarily for his contribution of ideas.

The Thinker

This person may be the quiet one in the room. Her problem-solving process starts with mulling over the problem, researching it, reflecting on it, and exploring different perspectives. She often uses brainstorms to take in new information, but she does her best ideation independently. The Thinker can easily support her idea with a well-thought-out rationale.

The Inventor

This person can think on his feet. He thrives when the pressure is high and timelines are tight. In the brainstorm room, he's often the one vibrating with ideas that he cannot wait to unleash on the world. The Inventor isn't afraid to push for big ideas or multiple concepts, but he doesn't always invest the time to fully understand the finer details surrounding the challenge.

The Producer
This person is the marathon runner of concept or product development. She has the stamina to shepherd a project through every phase. In the brainstorm room, she gets the group to build on promising ideas. When the dust settles, she continues to test out the chosen idea and explore different applications. When it's time to execute and others have grown bored with the project, the Producer still has energy to bring the idea to life.

When scheduling a brainstorm, assign different roles to participants — ones that are different from their normal brainstorming styles. Get big personalities to try the Thinker role, get the senior leader to become a Flag Bearer — you get the idea.

Hold a seeding brainstorm

One way to identify innovative and creative thinkers in your company is to host a seeding brainstorm. Depending on how ambitious you feel, present your problem to a department or to the whole company. Upcoming marketing campaigns, customer events, product prototypes, philanthropic initiatives, and company retreats are all good topics for a seeding brainstorm. Tell staff what kind of solutions you are looking for; you can be specific or broad depending on the type of ideas you're hoping to get back.

Hand out cards to everyone and request that they write, draw, or glue something onto the card. It can be anything that pops into mind when they think of your project. Ask staff members to tack their ideas up on a designated "idea wall" in the lunchroom or another common area. If you work with a remote team, share the challenge on your intranet or simply ask people to email their ideas to you to post on their behalf.

Make sure team members sign their cards so you know who is seeding each idea. It will give you a good indication of who's interested in ideation because they will participate fully and seed a lot of ideas to the wall. The heavy seeders are prime candidates for the innovator role in future matchmaking exercises, as they bring a lot of enthusiasm to projects.

You'll also learn who seeds the really different, out-there ideas. While their suggestions might not be viable for this particular project, stay connected with these folks. When you're stuck on a creative problem, you know the out-there idea people will help you consider some new angles and shake some new ideas loose.

Hold a junior consulting day

Consultants, for the most part, play an important role in a company's ability to innovate and problem solve. They can help you see new ideas and think about your business in different ways. They are also not hindered by your company politics or past transgressions. Junior employees have the same qualities, so take advantage of their untainted outlook while you can.

Try holding a junior consulting day or challenge. Give your junior team permission to evaluate your organization or department as a whole. Invite them to provide recommendations in the same way that a paid consultant would. You can evaluate their input and have your team implement any winning ideas.

Here are a few simple steps to hosting a junior consulting day:

1. Build a team by randomly picking junior staff from different departments.

2. Task them with one specific challenge. Quality of product, ideas, budgeting, planning, or structure are all prime areas for a junior consultant to consider. You might also want to issue an open call for general recommendations on improving the organization or department.

3. Brief them on the specific challenge. Let them know if there are any areas that are off limits (for best results, however, avoid setting limitations). Give your co-workers a heads up — junior consultants may want to meet with them to gather feedback.

4. Hold a question storm. After the briefing, invite the junior consultants to ask as many questions as they want. Be as open as possible when answering and try to keep any of your own biases in check.

5. Give the consultants time to work. Protect their schedules and give them a private space to work together, conduct their analyses, formulate ideas, and prepare their recommendations.

6. Hear their findings. Ask junior consultants to present their findings and recommendations to you and your department. Invite your supervisor to listen in — it will help everyone take the recommendations seriously and avoid the "We've tried that before" and "It won't work" excuses.

3.

STOP TRYING TO BE SO EFFICIENT

Monotony kills creativity,
so invest the time to shake things up.

> I don't want to take our designer off that project, because she knows it better than anyone else. Who cares that she is bored to tears working on it? When the team operates efficiently, we'll see greater returns.
> — Some Stooge Somewhere

Very few people can tolerate monotony in their personal lives. We quickly abandon monotonous gym routines, diets, hobbies, and relationships in favor of something more exciting and fulfilling. Yet we regularly tolerate monotony at work. Many organizational roles are designed to get people performing the same set of tasks over and over, year after year, because the company's bottom line loves an efficient team.

What few realize is that the highly productive, highly efficient team is only a short-term solution for your company's long-term need to continue delivering a quality product.

Repeating the same task has diminishing returns. You've probably had the following experience: You're assigned a new task. At first, you're frustrated because it feels slow and awkward. Once you start to get the hang of things, you feel more confident and start to enjoy the challenge. Each time you repeat the task, you get faster and faster. You feel a sense of satisfaction when you master it, and you enjoy that feeling for a short while. Then, the monotony sets in. You dread the task and want to get it over with as quickly as possible. You start taking shortcuts and the quality of the outcome slowly starts to deteriorate.

Many managers will tolerate this situation because they believe it is better to have an efficient employee who takes a few shortcuts than an inefficient employee who slows down the entire team. That's why we see so many creative teams set up like manufacturing lines. What worked for Henry Ford does not work for the development of creative ideas.

Giving "workers" or "doers" opportunities to innovate and create is necessary for maintaining the engagement and motivation they require to do quality work.

New challenges motivate creative people

An agriculture company hired a junior graphic designer for its marketing team. The designer had grown up on a farm and understood that audience. She also had a great college portfolio, a farm-girl work ethic, and a keen desire to contribute to a team.

Impressed by her zest, the director of marketing gave the designer one of the department's most tired projects — the annual report. This project hadn't seen a stitch of creativity for ten years. "What can you do to refresh this project?" the director asked the designer.

The designer accepted the challenge and set to work. She developed a fresh concept, updated the design, and applied a more vibrant voice to the content. The director was impressed and assigned all of the company report projects to the junior graphic designer. The director's hope was that the designer would maintain her high level of creativity while getting faster and faster at churning out reports. What actually happened was very different: the quality and creativity of the reports deteriorated as the designer lost motivation and engagement in the repetitive work.

Some staff in the agriculture company valued a stable, predictable work day. The graphic designer was not one of those people. It was the opportunity to continually tackle new challenges in innovative ways that refilled her creative tank. When the tank ran dry, she lost motivation, her work quality suffered, and her boss's plan backfired.

Focusing on efficiency is a Proximity Paradox

To be efficient is to able to accomplish a task in a way that uses the lowest amount of time and effort possible. It's when you focus only on the essential tasks that you reach an objective quickly and with low effort. Good, right? Not if you care about the quality of your creative output. Efficiency increases your proximity to the issue. It will cause you to lose sight of the larger objective and other, more creative ways to achieve it.

An efficiency focus also doesn't leave room for the mistakes that can lead to something novel. Scott Adams, the creator of the famous *Dilbert* comic and a man who describes himself as a hapless office worker and serial failure, writes extensively about this process in his book *How to Fail at Almost Everything and Still Win Big:*

> Over the years I have cultivated a unique relationship with failure. I invite it. I survive it. I appreciate it. And then I mug the shit out of it. Failure always brings something valuable with it. I don't let it leave until I extract that value. I have a long history of profiting from failure. My cartooning career, for

example, is a direct result of failing to succeed in the corporate environment.[27]

Artists know the value of failure. The lowest times reveal the most authentic and universal human experiences, the kind of experiences that inspire their work and make it relatable. Artists also know the danger of efficiency. They cannot continually produce the same caliber of piece and expect their audience to continue receiving it with the same enthusiasm. Audiences want to see evolution — they want more heart, more poignancy, more truth, more craftsmanship, or more artistry. No one hails their favorite playwright for being efficient.

Efficiency in an advertising agency

Typically, an ad agency's creative department is set up in a way that gets a group of people working consistently on the same client accounts. There's a creative director, art director, copywriter, graphic designer, and production designer assigned to each client. Each of those professionals learns the intricacies of the client's products and services, and they work to continually improve the quality of the marketing materials they deliver to the client each month.

This system works very well a lot of the time. The creative team gets familiar with the client's business and its budget, objectives, product pipeline, audiences, stakeholders, and regulations. They also form close relationships with the folks on the client's team. They learn what they like, what they dislike, their working habits, schedules, and interests. When the relationship is harmonious, the two teams — agency and client — feel respected and valued. They can develop great working partnerships.

Another benefit of this setup, and perhaps the most important one from a business standpoint, is that the creative team gets very efficient. They conquered the learning curve a year ago. Now, they can jump into the client's projects very quickly and produce good, consistent work that gives their agency a nice profit margin. But this model can backfire and create a Proximity Paradox when highly efficient team members burn out.

At some point, the agency creative team gets too close to the client. The client's fears become their fears, the client's limitations become their limitations. They can lose the outsider's perspective that originally made them effective at coming up with new, big-picture marketing ideas. We'll unpack this Proximity Paradox effect further in Chapter Nine.

Burnout can happen as a result of stress, but it can also happen from repetitive work. A person working on an assembly line suffers the physical wear and tear that comes from repeating the same movements over and over again. The creative people you find in agencies suffer a cognitive wear and tear. They originally pursued the agency life for the opportunity to work on a wide variety of projects and subjects, and that kind of work keeps them energized and feeling fulfilled. When they work on the same client account day in and day out, their creative brains take a beating.

It is possible to lose your creativity. Fortunately, according to author and neuroscientist Dr. Mandy Wintink, you can also get it back:

> Many more neurons exist in our brains when we are born than are believed to be necessary. But after birth, a lot of pruning goes on, by virtue of a 'use it or lose it' phenomenon. More neurons, and connections among those neurons, exist initially but many of those connections are lost when they are not supported or used. It's like having more than one road or path between points. With infrequent use, a city council might decide to no longer service the road less travelled. As a result, those roads get

less and less use. Once out of commission, those paths are more difficult to resurrect. Difficult, but not impossible.[28]

We'll share some strategies for resurrecting your brain's creative paths later in this chapter.

The dilemma facing the Creative Director

When I began to see the signs of burnout on my team, I knew I needed to act fast if I wanted to maintain our high standards for quality and creativity. At the same time, I needed to balance a number of agency and client expectations, and that list wasn't exactly short.

I had to think about productivity. Keeping the same people on the same accounts improves productivity in the short run, but long term, people get bored and start to slow down. How could I strike a balance and keep the overall team productive and maintain our profitably and margin?

I had to balance client expectations. I had a person on my team whom my client loved. They trusted her and appreciated how well she knew their brand, and for that reason, they often referred our agency to other businesses. How could I pull this person off the account without upsetting the client?

I had to make sure we maintained our quality of work. It's not easy to jump in with a new client and figure out the details of their marketing or design. Every good piece of marketing has two sides. One is the technical standards side. Remembering the right legalese, keeping the product trademarks up to date, following the client's writing conventions, choosing appropriate photography, and properly incorporating the brand colors and patterns is no small feat and takes time to master. When putting new team members on an account, you risk botching the client's brand standards.

The second is the ideas side. You need to strike a balance between what your client is *willing* to do and what your client *should* do. You want to constantly push the creative envelope, but you need to recognize that some brands are more conservative than others. If you push the client too far outside of their comfort zone, they can feel misunderstood and may take their business elsewhere.

I also had to make staff engagement and development a priority. Creative professionals feel affirmed when they do good work and gain the respect of a client. It feels really good. But there is another thing that contributes to their well-being, and that is development in their craft.

Ultimately, creatives are craftspeople. They want to continue to develop their skills and improve what they're able to create. If they can't do that in their jobs, they quickly lose confidence and motivation. You must strike a balance between keeping them engaged in the work and giving them the freedom to develop their craft.

You may not lead a team of advertising agency creatives, but since you're reading this book, you probably work with a team that needs to innovate and also appease different stakeholder groups. How do you help your team continuously generate new ideas while remaining efficient and reliable?

Shake up monotonous jobs

Some organizations have helped efficient employees avoid monotony by offering opportunities for personal growth experiences. For example, ad agency Iris offered a Life Swap program, where their staff traded everything from working at each other's desks to living in each other's apartments. It helped the agency recruit and retain top talent because their staff members valued the variety of work and working environments they could get from a career at Iris, and they felt that variety contributed to their creativity.

Professional services firm EY is another example. Since 2005, EY has dedicated its best resources — talented, experienced people — to improving the success of promising entrepreneurs in Latin America. The EY professionals have a chance to test their skills in a new industry and country, and the entrepreneurs get new ideas and strategies to grow their businesses in a way that positively affects the local economy.

EY works with the not-for-profit organization Endeavor to pair what they call EY Vantage Advisors with high-impact entrepreneurs. The advisors work with the entrepreneurs on projects that are designed to improve the integrity and effectiveness of their key business processes. The program has a significant impact — both on the EY advisors (by offering them a world-class professional growth opportunity) and on the Latin American entrepreneurs and their communities (by helping to stimulate economic growth).[29]

Havas swaps creative talent between offices

Havas is a multinational advertising and public relations company with offices in more than 100 countries around the world. In 2014, it introduced a program called Havas Lofts. This program gives the company's staff the opportunity to work in one of its agencies in a different international city for a month. Participants in the program can experience both living and working in a different culture.

Havas Lofts was developed by Patti Clifford (now Patti Clarke). She joined the company as its global chief talent officer after running her own consultancy business as well as spending twenty years in the credit reporting/debt collection industry. Not having an ad industry background, she came into Havas with a fresh set of eyes.

One of the first things Clifford noticed when she joined Havas was that talent wasn't being nurtured. "Advertising has a robust pipeline on the front end of recruitment. But once you are in, it falls off a cliff," she said. "Nurturing talent wasn't happening in a meaningful way."[30]

A creative or innovative business can't afford to have its talented staff getting bored or burning out. Retaining star employees and keeping them motivated is just as important as recruiting them in the first place.

Havas developed a job-swap program to create a new professional development opportunity for staff and to transfer knowledge, intellectual property, and experience between staff in different locations based on demand.

Candidates for the Havas Lofts program were nominated by their managers and then matched with suitable international agencies of the company. They were each also assigned a local coach to help mentor them during their job swaps. The coaches were responsible for immersing the job swappers into their agencies' culture, processes, and tools. The job swappers identified the learning outcomes they wanted to achieve from their experiences, and the coaches helped to facilitate those objectives.

Participants shared their experiences on a dedicated company blog and on social media sites for the program.

Because Havas Lofts was a training program, there were fewer international logistical issues to overcome. For example, visas aren't necessary and there generally aren't labor law restrictions. Of course, depending on where a job swap happens, there can be some language or cultural hurdles to overcome. But that was all part of the immersive experience that the Havas Lofts program created.

In the first phase of the program in late 2014, twenty Havas staff members took up the job-swap opportunity. Swaps were arranged between the company's New York, Paris, and London offices. In just four weeks, the Havas Lofts social media sites had more than 7,000 internal and external views, demonstrating the interest in the program.[31] In 2015, the program was expanded to include Latin America and Asia.[32]

By 2017, the program had 152 participants spending time across sixty-six Havas agencies in nineteen cities, including Madrid, Dusseldorf, Mexico, Sydney, Frankfurt, Prague, Buenos Aires, Milan, Shanghai, São Paulo, and San José. The program now runs twice each year.[33]

Patti Clifford reflected on the reasons for the success and popularity of the program:

> Havas Lofts is our mobility program. We're a big global network and we kind of broke the paradigm that you have to go live in one place for a year . . . Research shows that millennials are less interested in length of time associated with it so much as frequency.[34]
>
> The participants in these programs tell us over and over again that they gain so much by spending time with others from the network. We also hear a lot of great stories about how what they learn in these programs gets leveraged when they are back in their home offices — whether it be a tool, a process, or a connection to someone with a unique skill. These programs are creating a more global and connected workforce at Havas, which certainly benefits our clients.[35]

Other multinational marketing, advertising, and media agencies, such as Maxus, Iris, and The Marketing Store have implemented similar swap programs. Like Havas, they have found that it gives their staff valuable experience to develop their skills and outlook, which also helps each company with staff retention.[36] It's win/win, as these testimonials from both job swappers and employers indicate:

> Our average employee age is twenty-eight. Our employees are Gen Y and they have a real desire to be global citizens and work abroad. We previously didn't have a structured way of doing this. We've not solved it, but Maxus introduced a program last year where seventy people from forty-five different offices around the world, spend two weeks on exchange in another office.
>
> — Lindsay Pattison, CEO, Maxus[37]

> It's human nature to feel like there's something bigger and better out there, and employees these days are getting bombarded with calls from recruiters pitching the next big agency or brand opportunities . . . As agencies, we need to make sure that we understand our employees' career needs and are able to work with them to develop career paths that are nourishing and benefit the agency and client.
>
> — Sarah Aitken, former managing director, Iris[38]

> The experience here has accelerated my growth, both personally and professionally. I worked with some great people and gained a wealth of knowledge here, which I will carry with me throughout the rest of my career.
>
> — Josh Cornish, former senior design engineer, The Marketing Store[39]

The job swapping concept has even extended beyond intra-company arrangements for some smaller, independent advertising agencies. One example is the recent temporary job swap by creative directors of Australian agency DDI and the German-based Grabarz & Partner. The Australian creative director involved in the swap, Chris D'Arbon, reflected on the benefits both he and his company received from the experience:

> For me, a creative exchange represents something more than a 'work trip' for two creatives. It's about bringing down walls between players in the same game to discover the richness in each other's story. There no one way to do this thing we call creativity, so let's take Paul Arden's advice against coveting ideas.[40]

Paul Arden, who D'Arbon mentioned, was the creative director of Saatchi & Saatchi for many years and a best-selling author on advertising and motivation. In his book *It's Not How Good You Are, It's How Good You Want to Be*, he said that creatives should give away everything they know if they want more knowledge to come back to them.[41]

Other companies and industries are also experimenting with local job swapping, viewing it as a way to foster innovation within their organizations to gain competitive advantage. One example is Intuit, a financial software company. This company believes that the industrial-era notion of job specialization is no longer valid in the digital media world. Many job roles in contemporary organizations now regularly overlap.

This environment requires a flexible organizational structure. Intuit facilitates that via encouraging its staff to temporarily swap positions with people in other departments. The goal is to bring a fresh perspective to organizational projects. For example, a person involved with product development can swap roles with a person on the marketing team. The length of the swap is at the discretion of management.

An added benefit is that the people involved in the job swap gain a better understanding of how different roles within the organization can collaborate to drive success.

> Intuit does not believe that an employee's career trajectory is in one area. Just because you are awesome at finance, does not mean you can't be awesome at marketing . . . We don't want talent in a specific area of expertise for a long time. Instead, Intuit is placing its talent pool in uncomfortable situations. That's how you get innovation.
>
> — Cézanne Huq, former online acquisition leader at Intuit[42]

Technology multinational Cisco is another to have embraced the local job-swap philosophy. Cisco staff can apply for either a time or job-swap program. Both programs facilitate talent rotation and agility. The time-swap program allows staff to swap twenty percent of their time with another individual in the company for a defined period. The job-swap program allows for a complete role swap, either temporarily or permanently. The company believes that both programs encourage staff skill development and innovation.[43]

Another variation on the theme involves job swapping between customers and suppliers. Tesco and Coca-Cola recently implemented a job-swap initiative to foster collaboration in their supply-chain relationship.[44] Selected distribution and logistics staff in the two companies traded places for a year. The swap program brought fresh insights and understanding of the issues and challenges that both companies face in distributing their products.

The companies gained insights from both B2B (business-to-business) and B2C (business-to-consumer) perspectives.

> Our teams already worked closely together and had a strong relationship, but we knew we could never fully appreciate the challenges each other face without experiencing it firsthand. We wanted to do something radically different that would give us greater insight and have a lasting impact on the way we work as a team and with our suppliers.
> — Tony Mitchell, Tesco supply chain director[45]

Strategies for creating distance from workday monotony

Can you introduce a job-swap program in your organization? If you can, take a page from Havas and the other companies we profiled. If you can't, try these smaller initiatives instead.

Break up the monotony by getting people to switch roles, introducing creative activities to your routine, and carving out time for people to experiment with new skills. It may be less efficient in the short term, but it will snap people out of their proximity to efficient tasks and create an environment that supports the development of creative talent.

Appoint brand and vision champions

Earlier in this chapter, I shared my dilemma as the Creative Director of my team. My solution to balancing the expectations of the agency and clients, while also keeping the creatives happy and fulfilled, was to introduce two new responsibilities: brand champions and vision champions.

A brand champion is the person (or people) on a project who understands exactly what the brand can and can't do. They know the legalese, colors, fonts, lingo, trademarks, and approval process. They are responsible for staying connected to the client and making sure its marketing initiatives are successful.

A vision champion is the person (or people) who is responsible for the creative vision of the campaign. They have to innovate and look outside of the client's organization and industry for new trends and ideas. They are responsible for developing outstanding, boundary-pushing creative.

At the start of a project, assemble your team and assign vision champions and brand champions. Task the brand champions with understanding your needs and concerns and the overall direction of your organization. Task the vision champions with finding the most creative way to achieve the project goals. Set a date to bring everyone back together and get the vision champions to pitch their ideas to the brand champions. Choose the most innovative idea that will both fulfill the client's needs and achieve the project objectives, and then work together to execute it.

After every project is completed, acknowledge the success of the brand champions for delivering a successful project and keeping you on strategy. Acknowledge the vision champions for challenging the team's thinking and developing their creative craft.

Then, get the brand and vision champions to switch roles. The team that was responsible for brand intimacy can now have a chance to get inspired and develop its craft, and the former vision champions can take a turn safe-guarding the needs of the organization.

Switching roles gives everyone some freedom within an environment that is typically constraining. It challenges your team members to think creatively, develop their craft, and find new sources of inspiration, which will reduce burnout.

Practice divergent thinking

Efficiency becomes a Proximity Paradox when we continually solve a challenge the same way. One example is car advertising, where manufacturers solve the challenge of promoting their vehicles in the same templated way, year after year, model after model. They show the vehicle driving through a moody landscape that appeals to the target audience, and they pair it with a trendy song from an emerging artist.

It's an efficient way to solve the advertising challenge, but it's not creative. The ad won't stand out in the sea of competitors using a similar template for their own advertising.

Earlier, we touched on Dr. Mandy Wintink's research on the many different connections in the brain, and how we can lose some of the connections if we don't use them. Psychologists believe the connections in our frontal cortices are responsible for creativity. Dr. Wintink says we can maintain or rebuild the creative connections with divergent thinking.[46]

If you took a marketing or advertising program in school, you're probably familiar with the paper clip exercise. The goal is to come up with fifty different things you can do with a paper clip besides holding paper together. Hold a divergent-thinking brainstorm with your team on a monthly or quarterly basis. Over drinks or snacks at the office or at a laid-back location off-site, meet for an hour and come up with 100 different uses for a small, insignificant item.

Creative ideas can flow easily when we turn off the inner voice that says, "That's a stupid idea." Set a timer and challenge participants to fill a whiteboard in ten minutes or come up with a new use for the object every fifteen seconds. The inner voice won't have a chance to chime in when a timer is counting down. At the end of the session, run through all the ideas and celebrate the most unexpected and unusual uses for the item.

This exercise will help unleash the creativity of anyone tasked with innovation or problem solving because it forces us to make new connections between two ideas. If you can come up with 100 unusual connections between the idea of a paper clip and the idea of usefulness, you can come up with a novel way to promote your company's brand or products.

Swap projects with a partner organization

Most marketing departments have a set of time-honored projects that they work on every year: it could be an annual report, a product catalog, a scholarship awards banquet, or a sales summit. These projects are tedious for your in-house team, but they could be fresh fodder for an outside creative.

Find an organization in a completely different industry with a similar marketing cycle to your own. When the annual projects roll around, swap teams. For example, get the partner's designer to create your annual report, while your designer creates the partner organization's product catalog.

Project swaps are an easy way to keep team members fresh by giving them a chance to work with a different industry, medium, or set of brand standards.

Here are a few tips to set up your project swap for success:

- Pick straightforward projects that don't require a lot of back and forth between company departments. Projects with plenty of past examples are great candidates.
- Get both teams to sign a basic non-disclosure agreement to give everyone peace of mind.
- Write a creative brief that includes background information; a description of the audiences or stakeholders, project

objectives, or success metrics; a concept or creative inspiration; any important limitations (such as budget, timelines, production specs, etc.); and a list of deliverables.

- Stay organized. You should be able to give your outside partner a complete package of resources, such as a brand standards manual and supporting files, an approved copy deck, production templates, reference files, and a workback schedule with important dates.
- Meet regularly to review your outside partner's work and make sure they're on the right track.

Distance creators:
The Global Children's Designathon

Designathon Works is an organization that designs education programs for children. One of its most popular events is a Global Children's Designathon event. Children from all over the world converge in various cities for a day of creative thinking where they develop ideas to solve real-world problems. When you really want to blow the doors off creativity and innovation, Designathon's founder, Emer Beamer, recommends giving the challenge to children. We interviewed her to find out more.

Why are children in a good position to brainstorm solutions to big challenges?
Children are more engaged than most people take them to be. The motivation is there, and they are unencumbered by knowledge of things that don't work. They have the mindset of "Let's find a solution," and are not hampered by cynicism. They can make unusual and unexpected connections with the information and knowledge they have, and they can come up with ideas that work.

How does the brainstorming process work?
Our goal is to invite kids into their creative space. That way, they know they have permission to think as big and as crazy as they like, which is usually not invited in school.

I spent a lot of 2014 working out how kids can bottle their imaginations. I found that if a question is too open, they get demotivated and don't know where to start. If the question is too closed, it's not exciting for them.

To invite kids into their creative space, we developed a design canvas with a series of questions. It is set up like a board game that is playful and big enough that three or four kids can collaborate around the same canvas.

The first question to answer is, "What problem around water do you want to solve?" The theme for the 2017 Global Children's Designathon was "Water Issues." There are four main categories of water problems globally: too little water, too much water, habitats that are being lost for fish and animals, and water pollution. The kids started by agreeing on which of these issues they were most concerned about.

The second question is, "Who is affected by this problem?" This question gets kids thinking about human- or animal-centered design. It provides context and helps the kids relate to the person or animal that is suffering.

There are eight more questions that lead the children through associations, like, "What else does the problem make you think of?" And then, "What could you invent to solve this problem?"

We facilitate the brainstorms, because sometimes the children in a group can't agree. They might get excited about two different problems, and they need to focus on one. Sometimes the two problems are closely related, like water solutions for animals and floods. We ask them, "In what environment is that happening?" or "What are you seeing?" These prompts give kids triggers to talk about the problems further, and then they often see the connections themselves.

We've taught this process to teachers around the world, so when we have an event, we put out an open call to their schools. Teachers see it as a future education style, where kids use their creativity to solve global challenges.

Any child can do a Designathon brainstorm; the format works every time. We've held brainstorms with children in England, with children from disadvantaged backgrounds in Nairobi, with high-IQ children in Singapore, and with everyone in between. The children get super excited, get onto it, have a great time, and come up with interesting things.

What are some of the ideas that stood out to you?

In Dubai for our Global Children's Designathon event, some kids considered shooting rockets at meteorites to see if there is water there that we can mine. In Florida, the children were worried about floods following Hurricane Irma. They came up with a house with telescopic stilts. You can make the stilts longer or shorter depending on what's needed. Houses can go higher as the water gets higher.

We see a lot of children using smart technologies, and they presume it will offer a lot of capabilities in the future. In the Netherlands, children were concerned that dams would prevent fish from returning to the spawning areas where they needed to lay eggs. Dams are a good idea because they provide hydro-electricity, but they also make it difficult for fish to return to their natural habitats.

The children came up with an idea for a smart tube that would give fish a pathway through the dam. The tube was connected to a camera that would recognize fish as they approached and then open the doors to the tube. They imagined that the camera could also record data on fish populations, species, and migratory patterns, and therefore be used as a remote research area, too.

How is the brainstorming process different from adults?

Children are a little different from adults. The process itself isn't too different, but the rhythm is different. They come to our workshop and say, "I already have loads of ideas and just want to make them." We need to facilitate their attention and focus, which is different from adults. With adults, you supply them with coffee to get them going. With children, you have to calm them down and get them to focus.

Do you ever work with private companies?

We recently worked with the Water Authority in Amsterdam to

come up with two solutions for the city, which tends to have too much water.

The children came up with a pavement tile for streets and paths. It acts like a sponge to take extra water away rapidly. After a heavy rain, a tile section of the path collects the water. It seeps through several layers of filtration as gravity pulls it below ground. Then, a pump under the paths pumps the clean water to an above-ground faucet that pedestrians can use to access clean drinking water.

The Water Authority is going to prototype this idea and one other at scale in Amsterdam.

Are the collaborating organizations surprised by the ideas children come up with?

It's still quite hard for some adults to take children seriously. They think children are there to be educated, or they think it's cute. But once we start the process, they change their perspective.

We've done some research and asked adults questions like, "Did you have any preconceived ideas of what the children could come up with?" or "Did the children surprise you?" Across the board, they are surprised how much children know and how good their ideas are. And it's really fun, of course.

PART TWO:

CREATE DISTANCE FROM PROCESS

You've heard of flipping houses, but have you heard of flipping horses? It's the same concept — buy low and sell high. Just like house flippers, successful horse flippers have an eye for potential. They cruise classified ad websites and hang out in racetrack stable areas, looking for unwanted horses with the potential to become show-ring champions. The horse flippers often have their own stables and the skills to quickly train a horse for a new career.

And just like in the real estate game, horse flippers often stand to make the most profit when they fix up and resell the horse quickly.

My friend flips horses as a side hustle. She loves to take a retired racehorse and turn it into a beautiful riding horse for someone to love and enjoy. Her process is to buy the horse in the fall, get it looking its best, use the winter months to train it for a new career, and then sell it in the spring when the market is full of eager buyers. The process takes about seven months.

One time, my friend strayed from the process. She got a horse with a fun personality and beautiful looks, and when the spring rolled around, she didn't put it up for sale. Instead, she decided to keep it for a few more months. She thought if she could spend more time riding it and take it to a few competitions, she could get more money for the horse.

Unfortunately, the plan didn't pan out the way she had hoped. She developed the horse to the level she wanted, but the region experienced a drought that led to a massive hay shortage. It suddenly became very expensive to keep any horse — let alone a well-trained show horse.

I've seen many creative professionals experience the same effect with their work. They are precious with the project; they try to make it perfect before releasing it to the world. When they finally do, it falls flat. They get so wrapped up in the process of researching, perfecting, and planning their idea, it creates a Proximity Paradox. They lose sight of the fact that their idea was meant to address an unmet need, and while they're sitting on it, that need morphs into something else or is fulfilled by a competitor.

Gone are the days of the grand reveal and launch party. Perfection is overrated. If you're onto something, launch as soon as possible. In this section, we'll look at areas where we can get caught up in processes, and we'll share strategies to speed up ideation and action.

4.

TRUST YOURSELF BEFORE DATA

Listen to what your gut is telling you, because guts work faster than researchers.

Imagine a donkey that is equally hungry and thirsty is standing exactly midway between a stack of hay and a pail of water. Unable to make a rational decision as to whether it makes more sense to quench his thirst with the water or satiate his hunger with the hay, the donkey dies.

This story refers to a paradox in philosophy around the concept of free will. It's called Buridan's ass. If you're responsible for creativity or innovation in your company, you've probably felt the great pain in the ass of having to justify and rationalize your ideas. Higher-ups will ask you, "Have you tested this? Do you know it's true? What data have you collected?"

Companies have access to more information today than at any point in history. Data can be seductive; it lures us in with the promise of answers. For example, you can hire a company to cross-reference census data with media viewership data and statistics research to find out information like the average income for a postal code, the residents' debt loads, their value systems, the kind of cars they drive, and where they like to eat out.

You can also hire an expert to conduct a sophisticated focus group with a sample of your target audience, and in that session, participants will reveal exactly how they feel about your industry and organization. You can even hire an expert to follow people around on the internet, find out what sites they visit, what devices they're using, and exactly how much time they spend on social media during work hours.

If we don't know when to quit researching and start acting, we can quickly get stuck in a loop like Buridan's ass. Here's a loop we often see in marketing teams:

1. The team prepares the creative for a new advertising campaign and hires a research company to focus-test it.
2. A couple of focus group participants raise a concern that the marketing team hadn't considered. The team hires a second research company to poll a larger market segment to see if the concern is prevalent.
3. The poll reveals that a small yet respectable portion of the market shares the concern. The marketing team develops new creative for their advertising campaigns and tests it with another focus group.
4. Repeat steps two and three.

The cycle of researching, adjusting, and researching again can take place in all areas of business. It eventually creates an elephant-sized pool of data of which no one can make heads or tails. Marketing teams that get stuck in this loop will eventually put out an advertising campaign that does not offend anyone — and does not engage anyone, either. They've fallen victim to a form of Proximity Paradox called analysis paralysis.

Analysis paralysis is often the result of assuming the right answer will be clear once you've collected enough information. But you won't find the magic bullet by just scrutinizing numbers.

Research gives us permission to delay tougher decisions

We once worked with a marketing director at a big accounting firm who loved research. Over the course of a year, he would hire every top research firm in the area to uncover every minute detail he could about his customers. He ended up with a dozen different audience segments within 100 square miles. Then he sat down with us, handed over the stacks of paper and said, "Now build me a marketing strategy that uniquely targets each of these twelve audiences, speaks to their values, and solves their specific problems."

I've never been to the base of Mount Everest, but I imagine that staring up at that 29,000-foot ice wall and wondering where to even begin would be very similar to how I felt in that moment, staring at the mountain of research. The marketing director and his team felt the same way.

That level of detail might be helpful for a digital marketing expert about to invest several thousand dollars in a very precise and targeted Google search engine marketing campaign. That kind of expert would seize those stacks of paper and make magic happen. But this particular client had hired us because he had a brand problem. You couldn't distinguish his accounting firm from the dozens of competitors just beyond his doorstep. His awareness among customers was less than five percent, his customer retention rates were dropping, and growth had plateaued.

He needed something big to turn the ship around and rejuvenate his brand. Something that would signal to current and potential customers that exciting things were ahead.

In my experience, the best advertising campaigns aren't those that leverage data correlated to my postal code. The ads that really stick with me are often the ones that speak to a universal human value or struggle. While it's convenient to have specific product offers served up to you at the times and locations when you're ready to buy, these aren't the experiences that build brand loyalty.

The client believed that if he conducted enough research, that big solution would be laid bare. We realized the research was actually a crutch he was using to validate a larger decision that needed to be made regarding the company's brand and positioning. As long as he was busy conducting research, he could kick that larger brand decision down the road.

We eventually advised the client that there were a lot of cool directions we could take his marketing plan, but none came with a guarantee for success. Every time you put something out into the world, you take a risk that people won't like it. To use a hackneyed quote, "You miss 100 percent of the shots you don't take." At some point, you must pick either Buridan's stack of hay or pail of water and go for it. Otherwise, you will wither away and die.

The past does not predict the future

People tend to use hindsight and research to convince themselves that an unexpected event would have been predicted had all the data been in. Psychologists call this "hindsight bias."[47] But all the data will never be in. And data can only show you the past. People hope they can use data like a crystal ball to see into the future. We want to be sure about the things we are moving toward to prove competency.

We want to be sure our product has all the right features so customers will buy it. We want to be sure our advertising campaign is novel so it will win an award. We want to be sure the recommendations we put forward will work so the client will hire us again. We want to look good to our boss so we get a raise and a promotion. And we don't want to be the people at Pepsi's in-house advertising agency getting dragged over the coals for the Kendall Jenner commercial.[48]

So we turn to research for guidance, or we turn to focus groups for validation. But these sources can only tell us what has worked in the past or which product option would be best for focus group participants on that specific day at that specific time. They don't come with a guarantee that by the time your product or campaign goes to market, the world won't have changed in a way that renders it completely irrelevant, or worse, tasteless.

In *The Systems Bible*, John Gall says, "The current army is always fully prepared to fight the war of the past."[49] After the Second World War, the US army modernized and became ready to fight the same war. But then they ended up in the jungle and got their butts kicked by a low-budget army in conditions they had never anticipated. Fast-forward to 2003: the US has the perfect weapons and equipment to win the Vietnam War, and they are putting them to use in the desert.

Excessive research hurts

Excessive research keeps us looking to the past for a silver bullet, which is a wasted effort. It also diverts our time to analyzing data, rather than taking action.

For instance, the marketing director at that big accounting firm was using advertising campaign research as a scapegoat to delay decisions on larger organizational problems. His company had no retention strategy — when customers showed signs of leaving, and then left, no one followed up with them or tried to retain their business. The technology that the organization offered customers was badly outdated. Some frontline staff were poorly trained and could not guide existing customers to increasing the amount of business they did with the accounting firm.

For us, it was painfully clear that the organization would make more headway on its customer acquisition and retention goals if it took action to fix the three organizational service gaps. We had distance from the data. We could see that a customer retention plan and employee training were internal initiatives that the firm could implement for the cost of a manager's time, and that upgrading the technology would create more value than a spring advertising campaign.

Our client couldn't see that because he was too deep into the research. He was convinced he could use data from the past to validate a future advertising campaign, thereby ensuring its success. He was not convinced he could use data from the past to validate a series of service changes that would affect the entire company and its customers. The cost of a failed advertising campaign was about $150,000 in marketing budget. The cost of failed organizational changes was his job and reputation.

Sometimes, big innovation starts with a small step

It sucks to be wrong, but life is full of variables. Something will always happen that you can't account for. Some campaigns will flop, and some will be wildly successful — like Diamond Shreddies.

Minimize the pain of a flop by avoiding a big fall. Use existing data to choose one small action you can take immediately. Maybe the data suggested your customers prefer a different tone from your advertising — try it on one channel. Maybe it revealed a new niche audience — create a small campaign for them. Maybe it pointed you to a new prospective client or partner — take them for lunch. The cost of the failure is low, but if your action is successful, the value generated by the outcome is high.

You'll make more progress building the plane while flying it than you will staying in the hangar evaluating the parts.

Focusing on the customer problem led Apple to the iPod

Apple is famous for the brand loyalty it has engendered in its users over the years. The iPod is one of its resounding success stories. It revolutionized how people buy and listen to their favorite music. It also helped the music industry overcome a huge problem that was threatening the commercial viability of record companies: the free, illegal downloading of songs that was rampant in the late 1990s.

Intuitively, you might think that exhaustive market research contributed heavily to the iPod's successful development. But the late Steve Jobs, Apple's co-founder and former chairman and CEO, once famously said:

> Some people say, 'Give customers what they want.' But that's not my approach. Our job is to figure out what they're going to want before they do. I think Henry Ford once said, 'If I'd asked customers what they wanted, they would have told me, "A faster horse!"' People don't know what they want until you show it to them. That's why I never rely on market research. Our task is to read things that are not yet on the page.[50]

The success of the iPod as a new product hinged on encouraging users to download lots of songs from Apple's iTunes store. This would not only generate additional revenue for Apple, but also encourage people to listen to their favorite music on the iPod as often as possible.

During the development of the first iPod device, Apple built several early prototypes. It soon became apparent that one of the problematic features would be the scrolling function. The scrolling options available on the early iPod prototypes were either directional (D-) pads or simple up and down arrow keys.

Both methods were cumbersome for the user. The more songs you downloaded onto the early prototypes, the more time-consuming it was to scroll through them to find the ones you wanted to listen to. This was totally at odds with the positive experience Jobs craved for the users of Apple's products.

Scrolling was also a problem for existing competing products offered by Sony with its Walkman portable music product. Sony was the initial market leader in the digital music (mp3) player category. Other problems for the existing digital music players at the time were their size and song storage capacity. To make a device that could store a lot of songs, it needed to be quite large (i.e., not a handy device that you could put in your pocket and take everywhere with you).

Apple set about solving both these problems.

While Steve Jobs was not a believer in conducting market research to find out what customers wanted, he was very customer-focused in terms of product development. He liked product innovations to be groundbreaking and stylishly designed, but also intuitively easy and convenient for people to use.

That philosophy has allowed Apple to develop a range of stellar product innovations over the years, including the iPod.

During product development discussions about the scrolling problem in the iPod prototype, Apple's director of marketing, Phil Schiller, suggested a click-wheel interface, rather than the traditional D-pad or arrow methods. Apple's designers subsequently came up with a mechanical spinning wheel on the face of the next iPod prototype they developed. The wheel was positioned below the screen.

This scroll wheel had buttons surrounding it that allowed you to access the iPod's menu, as well as to rewind, fast-forward, play, and stop songs. It looked markedly different from the grid or linear navigational layouts of D-pads and arrow keys on earlier iPod prototypes and existing mp3 players. It was innovative, stylish, and easy to use, so it ticked all those boxes. But most importantly, the faster the wheel was spun, the quicker the device would scroll through the songs. Users could therefore navigate larger lists of songs more quickly. It solved the user-experience problem!

There were other benefits of the wheel, too. You could spin it with just one hand and even when you weren't looking at the device. That allowed you to scroll without taking your eyes off the road when you were driving, or when the device was in your pocket. It also made the iPod suitable for visually impaired users.

The scrolling wheel was being used for other non-related products from other organizations at the time, most notably a cordless phone developed by Bang & Olufsen. This phone had a small screen that enabled you to search a digital phone book that it contained. Its mechanical wheel allowed you to quickly scroll through the large number of listings that a typical phone book contains. Schiller had seen that Bang & Olufsen phone and suggested that the iPod designers develop a similar scroll wheel to solve the iPod's navigation problem.[51]

The other problem of the pocket-sized iPod's song storage capacity was solved by Toshiba's development of a 1.8-inch, high-capacity hard drive. They had developed it as a general prototype. Apple's chief engineer, Jon Rubinstein, was shown the prototype in a standard meeting with Toshiba during the development of the iPod. He immediately told Jobs that it was the breakthrough they needed to make a pocket-sized device. Standard hard drives used in laptops at the time were 2.5 inches. If they had been used instead, the iPod would have been too big to fit in your pocket. Jobs authorized a $10-million check to have exclusive rights to as many 1.8-inch hard drives as Toshiba could make.[52]

In October 2001, Jobs launched the first pocket-sized iPod device. It had a 1,000-song capacity, a 5GB hard drive, and it retailed for US$399. The initial reaction from critics was mixed, with most believing its price tag was too expensive to make a big impact with consumers.

But consumers soon began voting with their wallets. Within fourteen months, Apple sold 600,000 iPod devices.[53] Incredibly, it also sold twenty-five million songs through its iTunes Store over the same period.[54]

Individual songs were initially priced at ninety-nine cents, with Apple taking twenty-nine cents per song for its role in providing a secure digital distribution network. The iPod established the market for digital music, with users quickly showing a voracious appetite for paying for songs to legally download onto their iPod devices. And the more songs people downloaded, the more important the scroll-wheel navigational tool became.

The iPod was therefore critical in providing two revenue streams for the Apple: the sale of the device, plus ongoing revenue from the sale of songs. Its share price skyrocketed. On the day of the launch of the first-generation device, you could buy Apple shares for US$9.38. In just over two years, the share price more than tripled to $32.20.[55]

By the end of 2006, annual iPod sales of US$39.4 million accounted for forty percent of Apple's overall revenue.[56] Demand for iPods and iTunes songs continued to grow unabated for several years. While the wheel certainly wasn't the only reason that the iPod became an incredibly successful product, it contributed significantly to the device's ease of use and popularity.

The second-generation iPod device was launched in 2002, less than nine months after the first model was released. It had even more song storage capacity, as well as an important enhancement to the wheel. The mechanical version was replaced by one that was touch-sensitive, with the buttons outside of the wheel.

By the time the fourth-generation iPod was released in 2004, the buttons were built into the touch-sensitive wheel. This navigational tool became a key feature of other subsequent iPod models such as the Mini and the Nano.

Over time, technology and the way songs are distributed has

continued to evolve and change. The original Steve Jobs slogan for the first-generation iPod of "1,000 songs in your pocket" is no longer relevant. Today, you don't need to store songs on a device to be able to access and listen to them whenever you want.

Songs are now typically accessed via the cloud using subscription-based web streaming services (including Apple Music). And smartphones have become the dominant way of accessing music. The convenience of the scrolling wheel has been surpassed by scrolling with your finger instead. Of course, Apple quickly became a leader in the smartphone market as well, with the development of the iPhone.

Steve Jobs himself paid tribute to the importance of the iPod's click-wheel functionality when he launched the first iPhone back in 2007:

> So, we have been very lucky to have brought a few revolutionary user interfaces to the market in our time. First was the mouse. The second was the click wheel. And now, we're gonna bring multi-touch to the market.[57]

The sixth generation of the iPod, released in 2007, was the last to feature the click wheel for navigation. But the wheel functionality was an incredible breakthrough that solved a major problem when the original iPod was being developed. The idea is regarded as an iconic moment in the development of a revolutionary and very successful product. It came from understanding and anticipating a customer's potential problem in using the iPod device and being determined to solve it, rather than from market research. If they had listened to market data, Apple may have created a paid version of Napster and another SanDisk Sansa-type mp3 player with more storage.

At the time of the launch of the sixth-generation device, more than 100 million iPods had been sold, along with two-and-a-half billion songs.[58] The iPod was the clear market leader in the digital music player market, with more than seventy percent market share.[59] Although iPod sales have largely evaporated for Apple, the revenue it generates via songs streamed from Apple Music continues to provide the company with strong revenue. Apple Music has twenty-seven million paid subscribers and that number is growing rapidly.[60] And Apple's entry into the music market can be traced back to the success of the iPod.

Strategies for creating distance from the data

Maybe you haven't had enough time with your data to gain the insight you need to redesign your beta product, launch your national brand campaign, or write your next book. But chances are probably high that there are a few small things you can knock off today that can move you closer to your end goal.

Experiment with trends

"The future is no more predictable now than it was in the past," John Gall writes in *The Systems Bible*. "But you can at least take note of trends."[61]

Write down all the recent trends that you've noticed in your website analytics, Facebook engagement, or customer feedback. Choose the three that interest you most, and then ask yourself, "Where is the arrow pointing?" In what direction does that trend suggest you point your marketing? What opportunity is out there that you can take advantage of?

Based on that information, define two or three small marketing experiments that you will conduct to test those trends. Create a mini project plan with the following information:

- The facts on the trend
- Your interpretation of the trend and the opportunity it represents
- The details on your plan to capitalize on the trend
- A description of the target audience
- Your budget
- The date you will launch the campaign
- The date you will analyze results
- How you'll know if your interpretation is correct

Once you've made the plan, follow it. Don't overthink it and stall, and don't be premature in interpreting the results. Give your experiment time to run its course, and then analyze it on the planned date. Don't be late, either — feedback must be prompt if it's going to be useful. If one of your experiments materializes in the way you had hoped, you need to be quick to capitalize on it before the circumstances that are making it successful change.

Here's an example. When I was in college, I funded my beer budget by blogging and managing social media for an equine pharmaceuticals company. I created content around equine first aid and general horse health. One trend I noticed was that Facebook comments would spike when I shared riding and horse care ideas that only half of our followers agreed with.

I looked at where the arrow was pointing and guessed that I could increase engagement by making the company's Facebook page a place where horse owners could share their own experiences and opinions, and not just receive indisputable horse health-care tips.

I decided that once a month for four months I would write a blog post on topics about which my readers held strong opinions, like whether to put an insulated blanket on a horse in the winter or whether to vaccinate your horse. My audience was made up of women in their forties who kept a few horses on their own farm and rode for recreation. The budget for blogging and promoting Facebook posts would remain the same. I would analyze the results in four months' time.

As I predicted, the hot-button topic posts received the most engagement of all blog posts published in a month. Followers would weigh in with their own opinions, and then debate or agree with other commenters. Followers also shared the hot-button posts more than other posts, and the page's likes got a bump as well.

You don't need a lot of data, strategic planning, or budget to open up new opportunities for your product or brand. You just need to keep your eyes open for the trends bubbling on the fringes, and be willing to experiment with them.

Trust your gut and launch

You can be a marketer sitting on the creative for a new campaign, an engineer sitting on the designs for a new product, or an HR professional sitting on the curriculum for a new employee training program. Before you take your baby public, you're going to stall and ask yourself: Is it good enough? Will people like it? Will I look like an idiot? That's the Proximity Paradox directing your focus to the potential negative outcomes, and you lose sight of the larger good your product will bring to the world.

In the *Startup School* podcast, Seth Godin talks about the importance of launching. "It's so easy to become paralyzed in the pursuit of perfect that you end up not being good. You're so worried about launching in a spectacular way that you never do."[62]

If you're hit with a case of analysis paralysis, try this:

1. Pick one crazy idea that you've always wanted to try but have never had the courage to execute.

2. Choose one tiny, narrow audience that may appreciate that idea.
3. Allocate five percent of your available resources to taking the idea live.
4. Trust your gut.
5. Launch your crazy idea to the tiny audience and see what happens.

Step Four is the hardest. Liz Ryan, a longtime Fortune 500 HR senior vice-president, says when the stakes get high, people fear their intuition. They want the comfort of data to present a logical decision for them. Ryan says that our intuition — or gut — is our compass and survival coach, yet in business, we ignore the body and rely on the brain. Unfortunately, our brains lag behind what our guts already know.[63]

Ryan found that when her gut recoiled, the logical reason for her reaction would drop into her brain twelve to seventy-two hours later. Skip that long wait and instead learn to listen to your intuition in the moment. Tune into your emotions and physiological reactions. When you think about launching that crazy idea, does your heart pound, your palms sweat, and your adrenaline race? It's probably a cue that you're onto something important.

Turn off the inner yammer of logical reasons to kill your crazy idea, and instead, go for a walk. Focus your attention on where your physical reaction is coming from. Your body may be arming you with courage to step up, trust your gut, and launch your product even though the outcome is not certain.

Remember that all great success stories start with a rocky opening chapter. As LinkedIn founder Reid Hoffman said, "If you are not embarrassed by the first version of your product, you've launched too late."[64]

5.

DON'T BE PRECIOUS
WITH IDEAS

Share your work freely; anything kept under wraps inevitably stagnates.

> In the long history of humankind (and animal kind, too) those who learned to collaborate and improvise most effectively have prevailed.
> — Charles Darwin[65]

How many times have you walked by a co-worker's desk and seen him quickly minimize his window? He's working on something and it's not ready to be shown yet. He doesn't want you to see it until it's perfect, complete, and — let's face it — too late to make any major changes.

As creators and innovators, we pride ourselves on our own IP. We want to keep our techniques and ideas close and safe, because at the end of the day, they're what set us apart from the pack. We often fear that someone will steal our ideas, or worse yet, judge us on them before they are finished. But often, the closer we hold our ideas to our chests, the less opportunity we have to get the input that leads to great innovation. Being overly protective of our ideas creates a Proximity Paradox that actually undermines our ability to bring great work to life.

Fear of failure

At my first agency job, I was put on an account for a local soup kitchen/low-cost grocery store. It was an amazing organization that focused on empowering its patrons. It believed that while a customer may not be able to pay for his breakfast today, tomorrow he may be able to pay $0.25 for it. And when you're a paying customer, you deserve to have your breakfast cooked the way you like.

If the $0.25 breakfast customer asked for his eggs over-medium and they came out over-hard, he could send them back and have them cooked again. Being empowered to choose powerfully influences a person's mindset, and this organization believed it was the first step to helping people get back on their feet. Sounds like a pretty amazing client to serve, eh?

Obviously, I wanted to do a good job and come up with some amazing advertising for the soup kitchen/low-cost grocery store. My designer teammate and I came up with an idea to solicit potential donors' empathy by showing them what it feels like to walk into a grocery store when you have limited income.

We had originally wanted to find a grocery store in the community that would let us come in and multiply all the prices on their food items by ten. But an experiential campaign was a real stretch for a client with limited resources, employees, and time. So we attempted to make this same idea work in a print ad instead. The designer went on iStock and found some produce photography to use in our proof of concept, and then she Photoshopped new price stickers onto all the fruit and veggie baskets. I worked on making the body copy tell the perfect story to get an empathetic response from readers.

My teammate and I worried about getting the buy-in of our associate creative director (ACD) and creative director (CD). Their standards were high, and they had no problem sending work back to our desks if they felt it needed more time. To make the stakes even higher, both the CD and ACD had worked on the soup kitchen/low-cost grocery store account previously, and they were equally invested in the organization's success.

We were worried that our proof of concept wouldn't meet the ACD and CD's expectations, so we kept our heads down and powered on to make the print ad as beautiful as possible.

Friday rolled around — the day the ad was due. (I don't know why account people like to set due dates on Friday, but for whatever reason, they do.) We printed out our proof of concept and brought it into the creative director's office. He immediately saw the glaring errors that we missed due to our close proximity to our own work.

The ad didn't convey the organization's differentiator — the empowerment angle. In fact, our ad did the opposite: it made even regular people feel powerless against the rising cost of food. If you saw our ad in a newspaper alongside the weekly specials at your neighborhood grocery store, you'd be wildly confused.

I was hugely embarrassed, completely discouraged, and totally panicked, because I didn't know how we would be able to pull together another ad in a few hours. Needless to say, we missed our deadline. We also had to sit down with the account representative and creative leadership team, go through the ad again, explain how we couldn't salvage it, and ask for more time to come up with another idea.

There was a lot of kind yet firm lecturing about the importance of checking in early and often, of not being precious with the work, and of developing multiple ad concepts. I'd heard these principles many times before, but being a young copywriter with a hunger to prove myself, I held my idea close to my chest. I was convinced it was a good idea, I was afraid it would get shot down, and I believed I could show people the concept's merit if I spent enough time finessing it.

I was too close to my idea, and I couldn't see its flaws. I was also looking really, really hard for only its best features. If I had followed the check-in-early-and-check-in-often rule, I could have saved myself a lot of tears and embarrassment.

The stakes were high in my mind, but in the grand scheme of things, this was a relatively low-impact project. I'm glad I learned that lesson then and not down the line when I was working on larger campaigns.

Idea protectionism on a personal level

Idea protectionism is the concept of shielding our work from the input of other people. We see this happen a lot in the marketing and advertising space, and we find creative people are often trying to accomplish one of the following three goals:

1. Keep your spot on the creative pedestal

When a good writer shares her first draft with you, it's a ruse. She's actually sharing her third or fourth draft. Most first drafts are so horrid, the writer shreds them so peers will never stumble across them. Writers fear that you will think less of them if you realize that their creative process is as messy as anyone else's.

Even though most brilliant ideas are born from the muck of hundreds of bad ones, creative people try to hide the fact that they must first fill the swamp. It's because we want to be judged by our good ideas — not our boring, clichéd, platitudinous, stupid, confusing, or demented ones. We maintain our position on the creative pedestal by keeping up the ruse that the majority of our ideas are good, not garbage.

2. *Command top dollar*

Over time, a creative person's process for filling the swamp and conceiving good ideas gets faster and faster. You develop your own mental tricks, hacks, and processes to speed up the process. And that's important because the time required to come up with ideas is inversely proportional to compensation — the less time you need, the more salary you can command. That's why a top designer charges thousands of dollars for a logo and completes it in two days, while a junior designer charges hundreds of dollars and takes four weeks.

Your process for producing great ideas quickly gives you a competitive advantage over other creatives. By letting others see your process, there's a risk they'll copy it, rise to your level of ability, and then compete with you for compensation.

3. *Avoid the stress of accountability*

When we tell others that we're working on a new idea, a few days later, something terrible happens: They ask us how it's going. We want to slap them, because it's probably not going well.

The scariest part about telling someone you're going to do something is actually doing it.

If we never share our ideas with others, and we fail to produce something good, we never have to admit that failure to anyone but ourselves.

The paradox of the three goals of idea protectionism is that in trying to protect your position, compensation, and reputation, you build a fence that locks you in as much as it keeps others out.

Idea protectionism can limit your ability to innovate and come up with new ideas. That's because it prevents others from providing feedback that could steer you down a new path to better ideas. It keeps you rooted in your current way of doing things so you never grow. It lets you stay in your comfort zone and avoid being held accountable to achieving your full potential.

Idea protectionism has bystanders

Have you ever worked with someone who keeps all his ideas to himself? How do you feel? You probably assume that person is too snobby to tell you about his project, or that he thinks you are stupid and won't have anything to offer. Even worse is when this person finally does reveal the finished product, and you can see it's terrible, but you're either too kind or too shy to tell him so.

In an advertising agency or marketing department, there are two groups of bystanders to idea protectionism. The first group is your fellow creatives — the ones who won't get a chance to collaborate and grow, and who will have idea protectionism modeled as an acceptable way to work.

The second group is made up of clients or other departments in your organization. What they want is a bunch of good ideas from which to choose, and they're OK with a rough package at the early stage. What idea protectionists sometimes deliver is one bad idea in a beautiful package and no additional choices. The client might end up being the one who has to break the news that your idea sucks, and that negatively affects your relationship and the reputation of your agency or department.

Idea protectionism on an organizational level

In some industries, it can take decades of work and billions of dollars to bring a new product to market. It's getting more and more costly to develop IP, so it's no wonder companies want to protect it so closely.

We've worked with a lot of organizations in the agriculture industry, and that has to be one of the most costly and competitive spaces for innovation. In the last decade, the cost to discover, develop, and implement a new plant biotechnology trait was US$136 million. The time from initiating the development project to launching the plant trait was 13.1 years on average.[66] To put that into perspective, complex apps cost about $1 million to develop.[67] App developers can typically get version 1.0 built in six months.[68]

Agriculture organizations and others that operate in expensive, competitive spaces have operationalized the protection of ideas. The innovation teams work in a separate facility with an address that is kept under wraps. Employees cannot use any external memory devices on their machines, such as USB drives, to add or remove files. Every employee and partner signs a mile-long non-disclosure agreement. The legal department is consulted on every communications piece, no matter how small.

All of these protocols keep the company's valuable IP out of the hands of competitors or malicious people who would seek to damage the company. But the harsh truth is that NDAs and patents are hindering our ability to create something our customers really love. The firewalling directs our focus to protecting what we've got, rather than looking ahead and asking, "What's next?" Or, "How can I now make this product irrelevant?" It cultivates an intense proximity that undermines innovation.

Look at Kickstarter. Entrepreneurs lay bare their ideas for others to see. Yes, there's a risk that someone will swoop in and steal a great idea (and they do), but there's an even greater opportunity for the entrepreneur to collect valuable input, build momentum toward launch, and create a community of loyal customers and advocates.

How Pebble built a community by openly sharing ideas on Kickstarter

Pebble was a smartwatch company that enjoyed spectacular success in developing and financing its product idea via the Kickstarter crowdfunding platform.

Let's look at how it all unfolded.

Smartwatches are a relatively recent product innovation. When Pebble was looking to enter this new market, so, too, were many competitors like Fitbit, Under Armour, Garmin, Apple, and Jawbone. The temptation for Pebble to keep its ideas very close to its chest was high, as it is with any groundbreaking product innovations.

The initial development of successful technology products is notoriously expensive, with much trial and error along the way. And there's certainly no guarantee that technology product ideas will ever even be launched, let alone be commercially successful. This can make potential investors very wary of committing their funds. It's high risk, with the possibility that investors will either lose all their money or only receive a minimal return. And for every technology investment success story, there are plenty of failures.

Pebble initially tried to attract funding via the traditional means of raising venture capital — from wealthy investors, financial institutions, and other potentially interested firms. But it failed to attract the level of funding it needed.[69] Without the necessary funding, Pebble could not emerge from the starting gates.

Like smartwatches, the concept of crowdfunding is a relatively recent phenomenon. Instead of attracting large investments from just a few investors (like the venture capital approach), it seeks to raise small amounts of money from a lot of investors, using the power and reach of the internet.

The potential downside of using a crowdfunding approach is that your idea is very publicly exposed. There is the risk that it can be stolen, adapted, or exploited first by others. But there are also potential upsides — it can help you to obtain the funding you wouldn't otherwise be able to generate, and it can establish a community of people who are interested in your idea.

We now know that a Kickstarter community can do a lot more than financially support your idea — it can also offer feedback to help you develop your idea further. The community members can also become your first buyers and promoters when your product idea is launched. You can secure long-term customer support and loyalty by listening to your community's feedback and acting on it.

We now know this about Kickstarter communities because Pebble proved it.

Whether it was by chance or necessity, Pebble provides a perfect example of making an innovative idea very public via the crowdfunding approach. And it's certainly arguable that publicly revealing its idea well before its smartwatch models were produced and launched was the major reason why the fledgling company shone so brightly in the early years of the wearable technology market.

Pebble decided to use Kickstarter as its crowdfunding platform in April 2012. Its initial goal was to raise US$100,000 within thirty-seven days. To entice investors, they were promised a discounted Pebble smartwatch as soon as the product could be developed. The more that investors donated, the greater the discount they would receive on different models in the planned Pebble smartwatch range.

Proposed features of the Pebble watch models included the ability to download apps and to link the watch to iPhone and Android smartphones via Bluetooth. The watch would then silently vibrate when the wearer received voicemail, text, email, or social media messages. Other proposed functionality on more premium models included the ability to track fitness data like the speed and distance traveled when exercising.

It's important to gain early momentum in a crowdfunding campaign, but the initial results for Pebble were staggering. Within two hours, it had reached its fundraising target of $100,000. Within twelve hours, it had raised $500,000.

Kickstarter had been operating since 2009. Before Pebble, the fundraising record for an individual campaign was $3 million in sixty days by a video game producer.[70] Pebble broke this record in just six days, and by the time its campaign had finished, it had attracted 68,929 backers pledging more than $10 million![71]

The success of the Kickstarter crowdfunding approach put Pebble's smartwatch firmly in the public domain. It allowed the fledgling start-up to gather ideas and build momentum with an online community. And that community was prepared to offer feedback and support its smartwatch ideas.

The Kickstarter campaign also delivered another somewhat unexpected but important additional benefit. Within days of the launch of the Kickstarter campaign, company founder Eric Migicovsky revealed that he was being deluged with hundreds of emails:

> People want to know every detail about the watch and figure out what sort of apps they can make for that. It is really causing people to stop and think, 'What would be a cool thing, what would be a useful thing to run on my watch?'[72]

The campaign was therefore encouraging developers to create apps for Pebble's smartwatches to enhance their functionality. It spurred the company to think creatively about potential use scenarios and to develop associated apps. These apps subsequently became an important, ongoing feature of Pebble's smartphone models. The company fully embraced the notion that being open about ideas leads to enhanced product development.

Migicovsky articulated this philosophy in the following statement:

> Our developer community set Pebble's wearable technology ecosystem apart from the rest. No other wearable platform was more open or gave developers more freedom to create, experiment, and delight the world with beautiful watch faces, useful apps,

and unique experiences. The Pebble Dev community's mission was to Make Awesome Happen, and
they accomplished that beyond our wildest dreams.[73]

Pebble put its IP out to the world via Kickstarter, and many people came back with additional smartwatch features that they wanted to see. The company subsequently worked hard to integrate those features into its smartwatch model development to give its backers what they wanted. Pebble wouldn't have come up with as many enhancements if it had taken the approach of developing its smartwatch in isolation in a lab and waited to unveil it at a grand event.

Pebble brought a new dimension to crowdfunding. It's no longer a means to fund product development; it's also a platform to build a community of like-minded individuals and rally them around a vision for a product. The community creates leverage that the company can use for ongoing product development and support.

The initial Pebble Kickstarter campaign ended in May 2012. The company then embarked on the development and mass production of its initial range of smartwatch models. They were first available for sale in July 2013. By the end of 2014, Pebble had sold more than one million smartwatches.[74]

Buoyed by the success of its initial Kickstarter campaign, the company used the platform twice more to test and promote its ideas for subsequent models. These campaigns were also massively oversubscribed and broke records.[75][76]

Given the excitement and funding Pebble generated via the Kickstarter crowdfunding community, you might expect that the ongoing financial success of the company was guaranteed. But after two years of profitability, the company began accumulating losses. It never recovered and eventually filed for insolvency.

Despite its operational demise, its assets and many of its staff were acquired by Fitbit, one of its major competitors. Fitbit paid

US$23 million for Pebble's intellectual property.[77] This included its smartwatch operating system, apps, and patents. Its ideas were its major asset, even though the company was in liquidation.

One of the major reasons cited for Pebble's operational demise is that demand for smartwatches as a specialist product category didn't reach a critical mass quickly enough to sustain all the market competitors that quickly emerged. That made it difficult for an organization like Pebble to sustain its commercial viability, given it focused exclusively on this category.[78]

Smartwatch competitors like Apple have more diversified revenue streams and are therefore less dependent on a single product category. This allows them to ride out competitive situations in the early years of crowded, less mature product categories. These markets invariably have more potential for revenue fluctuations, as Pebble discovered.

However, the key takeaway from this case is that Pebble developed extremely valuable IP, largely due to not keeping its ideas locked away during product development. Fitbit can certainly see the potential in that IP. The company has a broader range of wearable products that should be able to leverage it. Not many (if any) liquidated companies receive $23-million offers for their IP like Pebble did.

And the value of that IP was significantly enhanced by the open way that the company developed its ideas. You could argue that without that approach, Pebble would not have had any significant assets to sell when the end came.

Strategies for creating distance from your products and ideas

This first step to overcoming idea protectionism on a personal level is simple but not easy. It requires convincing yourself that your creative output on any given day does not reflect the sum total of your creative abilities. Some of your ideas will suck, but that doesn't mean you suck. Some people will crap on your work, but that doesn't mean they think you're crap. And if they do, they're probably not great people themselves.

When you put your ideas out to co-workers, customers, or the world, be cool with them. Embrace the praise, criticism, and suggestions that will give your ideas life outside the confines of your mind.

When sending a video script out for feedback, I like to give it a new name, like, "The Courage Story," rather than, "My video script for the university." It helps me create distance in my relationship with the script so I can accept feedback objectively and let the script take on a life of its own.

It's also important to remember that art and creativity is subjective. A friend of mine often says that if fifty percent of people who see your work don't like it, then it wasn't good to begin with. In marketing, we often say that when you try to please everyone, you appeal to no one. Accept the fact that your idea will have some haters, and remember that it's no reflection on you or your talent. You're going to go on creating long after the current project is dead and gone.

Adopt a growth mindset for your brand or products

In her book *Mindset*, psychologist Carol Dweck compares a fixed mindset to a growth mindset. People with a fixed mindset believe that qualities like their intelligence or talent are fixed. People with a growth mindset, on the other hand, believe that that their intelligence and talent can be continually developed and improved.[79]

On a personal level, choose a growth mindset. Break free from the fixed mindset that makes you feel that your intelligence and abilities are up for judgment. Reframe the way you view challenges and hardships. Instead of greeting them with dread, greet them with optimism and anticipation. Creative people grow fastest when they push themselves to the edge of their ability, fail, get up, and move forward.

On an organizational level, make collecting positive and negative feedback a priority in your creative or product development process. You can have a drink and lament the bullies later. As soon as you have the concept together, share it with stakeholders. For highly specialized IP, bring together a small group of people you admire and will share honest feedback. For IP that can be appreciated by a large group of people, consider sharing it and gathering feedback through online forums, surveys, and crowdfunding platforms.

The key here is to get feedback early and often. Don't schedule the first check-in after you've spent half your budget or taken the project nearly to completion. It's hard to change or adjust the course once you've made the stakes impossibly high. It's easy to accept feedback when you still have the freedom to nimbly change course.

One of the most basic things a marketing department or advertising agency can do to operationalize feedback-gathering is to put work-in-progress up on a wall. Pick a wall that's well trafficked by staff, but not by clients.

As soon as you have the concept together for a campaign, video, landing page, customer event, or anything new, put it on the wall. Pencil sketches and snapshots of whiteboard drawings are sufficient for expressing the idea in the concept development stage. Keep sticky notes and pens near the wall and invite all staff to contribute feedback. Check the wall for feedback regularly and post new iterations of the concept as you build it out.

Create a fail board

We've been fortunate to work with Balmoral Hall School, an amazing all-girls school in our hometown. One of the things that makes this school so amazing is its attitude toward failure. The faculty teach students to embrace failure, not fear it, because it's only by pushing yourself to the edge that you learn what you're truly capable of. When students try and fail, they're praised for their courage and supported in taking their learnings and trying again. The students become confident women who don't let a fear of failure stop them from pursuing their interests.

There's a lot that marketers can learn from these students.

Pick one upcoming work project at which you would be willing to fail. A low-cost project with a longer timeline, few stakeholders, and opportunities to try a new craft, technology, rollout, or strategy makes an ideal test subject.

Then, up the ante for the project and try to push yourself to your limit. For example, can you remove features to move up the launch date? Can you add features and make your product ten times better than the competitor's? Is there a different platform to carry your product? Explore avenues that are outside the zone of what you know you can deliver.

Next, install a fail board in your workspace. When the project goes sideways (as you expected it would), document mistakes and failures on the board. Attach a note of learnings to each one.

Invite your co-workers to participate by creating their own fail boards. Host a quarterly failure awards show, where everyone gathers together to share their failures and learnings freely. Award prizes to the setbacks that ultimately led your team to some form of success (such as developing expertise in a new area, improving a process, redefining a goal, etc.).

Most importantly, give others the chance to use your failures as a springboard for their growth and development.

Launch a (potentially) doomed venture

Think the fail board is child's play? Try this. Conquer idea protectionism by launching a venture that is likely to fail. Have you ever had a silly idea for a game, book, t-shirt, app, or online store? Build it! (But don't blow your life savings on it. You're making an investment in the process, after all, not the product.)

I once paid a designer to develop a smartphone sticker pack. I set up my company, registered it in iTunes, and challenged myself to market the idea. Then I failed. Hard.

It all started when I saw a stat that said the poop emoji was one of the most popular emojis available. So I figured, let's give the people what they want: more poop. Enter Pooporium, the ultimate stinky sticker collection! Because if you can't say it with poop, then you shouldn't say it at all.

I launched an app of realistic poop stickers on iTunes. Or I tried to, anyway. The iTunes representative assigned to my account was pretty grossed out and did not accept my sticker pack, no matter how many times I tried to change her mind. Only slightly discouraged, I submitted my sticker pack to the Google Play store. They cleared it for publishing.

So far, Pooporium has not been the overnight success I hoped it would be. Instead of a million downloads, it's had five. So why launch a potentially terrible idea? Because you bring your idea to market quickly, avoid getting hung up on the details, and learn a lot through the process.

With Pooporium, for example, I created something that five people may really like. Likely, they're tween boys. But still, if I didn't go through the process of setting up the Pooporium business, I may not have started my own agency, just a few months later. I saw how easy it was to get started and realized there wasn't any magic to launching a new venture.

To launch a mini-venture, all you need to do is:

1. Choose a budget. Keep it small. Consider the expense an employee development cost or continuing education investment.

2. Come up with an idea. It should relate to your industry, but the connection can be loose (insert gross poop joke here).
3. Set a deadline. The sooner you can get your product to market, the better. Delays will kill your enthusiasm and interest in the product.
4. Go through the motions. Identify the steps needed to bring your idea to life, such as establishing a corporation, hiring a manufacturer, or submitting a proposal. Then sit down and make it happen. .
5. Ignore the voices in your head that provide you very real and rational reasons to stop. You'll hit a point where you get busy with other work, and your foolish product launch will seem just that — foolish. Don't give up. Quitting now will only make the next attempt that much harder.
6. Cross the finish line and celebrate the success or failure of your new initiative.
7. Plan your next venture. Or, if you get lucky, retire on the success of your first one. Just don't get your hopes up too high.

6.

COME UP WITH
IDEAS TO PLAN

Make creativity today's priority; don't waste time building a plan to address it later.

North Americans spend about fifty-five percent of their working hours on meetings, administrative tasks, and other "interruptions" from their primary responsibilities.[80]

I came from a company that spent a lot of time in meetings — planning meetings, to be more specific. The company encouraged a high level of involvement in internal meetings to better the organization.

I was responsible for a team of managers who were tasked with creativity. They needed to bring together new and innovative ideas on a daily basis. I often received complaints from my team about a lack of focus time, which made it difficult to come up with good ideas and create new things. They felt like they were spending all their time planning the next project or catching up on existing ones. To stay on top of things, many of them had to do their ideation outside of working hours.

I asked my team to write down all the meetings they had with their own teams and to provide me with the list. I wanted to see the extent of the problem. The list confirmed that we certainly had a problem. The managers spent about fifteen hours a week on internal meetings.

The three meeting motivators

Why is it we often feel we need to do our best creative work outside the nine-to-five workday? Why are those hours so much more productive, so much more creative? The truth is they're not. We've trained our brains to no longer see these beautiful eight-hour stretches of time as a chance to do anything meaningful.

Instead, we see our days as cesspools of interruptions and meetings. We pack our calendars with redundancy — meetings where we kick a project down the road or talk about what we've got to do next.

I believe there are a few reasons why teams meet so much, and none of them are good:

- Doing the actual creative work is difficult. We meet because it's often easier than putting in the work to create something new.
- We want to avoid personal responsibility for the work. When we meet, a group of people can talk about doing something rather than actually doing it.
- We believe meetings lead us to better results. This is very debatable.

Imagine if you took all that wasted time and turned it into creative thinking and action instead. If I told you that you could have eight hours of time today, all to yourself to think, create, and innovate, it would probably be a dream come true.

Bad meetings are a plague for companies

Unproductive or prolonged meetings can become a virus that affects an entire organization. It infects the organizational culture and becomes especially difficult to overcome in large companies.

Ironically, advances in technology have arguably made meetings harder to avoid in the contemporary workplace. We can theoretically be contacted 24/7 by local and international colleagues and clients. And we can attend meetings remotely using our smartphones and video conferencing technology.

Being out of the office or traveling in another time zone are no longer convenient excuses to skip meetings. The modern employee can waste time from anywhere.

Meetings can become a crutch

Some organizations (and some staff members) can become so used to a meeting culture that they believe their company cannot function without regular meetings. If this is the philosophy of the senior management of an organization, it can become impossible to shift the mindset of the staff.

If you or your team are constantly distracted by this type of bureaucracy, your creativity will inevitably suffer.

You need to truly value your time and the time of your team. Not in a financial sense, but using the economic principle of opportunity cost. In other words, any time that you waste in unnecessary or prolonged meetings is time that you could potentially spend doing more creative and productive tasks at work.

Completing important tasks outside of work hours is not a viable alternative. While the after-hours approach might enable you or your team to temporarily stay on top of workload, it isn't sustainable for creativity and innovation over the long term. Your creativity will drop. Or you'll burn out. Or both of those things will happen.

Procrastination can be the core of meeting-heavy cultures

I remember sitting in a meeting to discuss a campaign strategy that the creative and accounts team were going to be putting together. The meeting had been called by one of our accounts people, who scheduled 60 minutes for a group of six of people.

We spent the first twenty minutes talking about the tasks that needed to get done. It took the equivalent of two hours of combined brain time.

We figured out what we needed to hold a 30-minute, deep-dive session into a client strategy, and then come up with a solution for the client's challenge.

Then we started to plan our next meeting to do the deep-dive session. I was thrown for a loop. Our one-hour meeting had started at 2 p.m. It was now 2:25 p.m. Instead of cracking the whip and using the remaining thirty-five minutes to do the deep dive, we were planning to schedule another thirty-minute meeting to solve the problem later!

At this point, I spoke up. I asked the group, a) What the heck? And, b) Why were we doing what we were doing? The response I got suggested that, at the core, we were procrastinating.

I am not saying I don't procrastinate. And, I am not saying meetings don't have a place in creativity. They absolutely do. They can be amazing tools for planning, brainstorming together, and getting a team on the same page. But they need to lead to action. They can't allow people to talk in circles and waste time. Unfortunately, in most companies, that's often what happens. Meetings delay progress.

The importance of a "doing philosophy" is summed up perfectly in this quote from Johann Wolfgang von Goethe, one of the greatest creative minds of all time, "Knowing is not enough; we must apply. Being willing is not enough; we must do."

Planning to come up with ideas versus coming up with ideas to plan

We kick creativity down the road when we schedule a meeting, bring a group together, talk about projects goals, and then schedule another meeting to brainstorm ways to achieve those goals. If you're an in-house marketer, does your annual calendar look like this?

- April: Develop sponsorship concept for summer
- July: Develop fall campaign concept and begin production
- October: Brainstorm ideas for winter campaign

Chances are probably good that you populated this calendar during an annual meeting to plan the marketing year. As marketers, we tend to kick creativity down the road. We create a calendar with small boxes of time and opportunity, and when the scheduled brainstorm rolls around, we force our ideas to fit into the box we created months earlier.

How would your marketing year change if you used that annual meeting to brainstorm bold new ideas for your brand or product? If you could pursue any idea — not just the one that fit into the predefined box — could you create more effective campaigns? We bet you could.

We need to shift our mindset to one where we make brainstorming great ideas our first priority. Planning to execute those ideas can come second.

Internal hackathons make continuous innovation a priority for Shutterstock

A large company that's managed to consistently unlock innovation is Shutterstock, one of the world's leading stock photography, video footage, and music providers. Since it was founded by entrepreneur and CEO Jon Oringer in 2003, Shutterstock has cultivated a culture of "intrapreneurship" within its organization. That means it allows its staff to act like entrepreneurs within the company.

Shutterstock staff members have the freedom to pursue innovative opportunities, just like Oringer himself did to establish the company. This approach helps to keep Shutterstock at the forefront of digital innovation. It also increases the job satisfaction of its creative staff, making it less likely that they will leave to establish their own start-ups or go to work for a competitor.

In the early 2000s, Oringer realized that there was a gap in the digital photography market. It was difficult to find royalty-free images online that you could subsequently use in your own creative commercial work. So, he began taking as many photos as he could, and eventually uploaded more than 30,000 of his own images to start Shutterstock. Advertisers were the bulk of his early customers, paying yearly subscriptions to download multiple images.

Shutterstock needed to quickly reach a critical mass of both subscribers and images to make its service viable. When it did, its need for innovation couldn't stop there. Continuous innovation is essential in the fast-paced and highly competitive digital industry in which Shutterstock competes. Oringer himself recognizes this challenge: "As we continue to grow, the question is, how do you keep the company as innovative as it was 15 employees ago?"[81]

This intrapreneurial philosophy makes it easier for Shutterstock to both attract and retain the talented people the company needs to survive and thrive. The company's leaders believe that they need to create an environment where innovative ideas can quickly come to the surface, without being stifled.

Since 2011, the company has hosted annual twenty-four-hour hackathons.[82] These events are held to encourage staff to pursue any creative ideas they have that could improve Shutterstock's products and/or give its customers a better experience. The innovative ideas don't have to be technical. For example, they can be marketing campaigns or recruitment initiatives.

Staff form teams to collaborate and work on ideas they are passionate about, with many literally working around the clock. All the organizers really need to do is to make sure there is plenty of food, caffeine, and energy drinks on hand for the hackathon event. The goal is for Shutterstock staff to develop ideas or quickly build rough products (hacks). Giant twenty-four-hour countdown clocks are projected onto the walls to add to the atmosphere. The theory is that this time pressure encourages creativity and decision making.

All Shutterstock staff can participate in the hackathons. Teams must include members from at least three different organizational departments as well as people who may not normally work closely together. The philosophy is that a good idea can potentially come from anywhere. Oringer is a big supporter of the hackathon concept:

> We have hackathons, which are pretty fun. A lot of people get really excited about them, and they can build whatever they want for the company — it could be crazy, practical, whatever. We actually wind up implementing a lot of those things throughout the year. It pushes a lot of thinking. It's pretty amazing what people can get done in twenty-four hours. Sometimes we talk about a new product feature, and it can take three months to build. Then someone

will prototype it overnight. Sometimes as a company you tend to overthink things. If you just sit down and try to do it, it turns out to maybe be easier than setting up meeting after meeting to get it done. So it's a good reset point for us every year to remind us, 'Yeah, we can just get things done quickly.'[83]

At the end of each hackathon, each team makes a short presentation to reveal its idea to the rest of their Shutterstock peers. The best ideas win prizes and receive further exploration in subsequent months to determine if they can become a viable new product or service offering for Shutterstock.

Engineer Dave Kozma has been part of a team that won the major prize during a Shutterstock hackathon. He has three tips for success during these types of events[84]:

1. Have a team plan. This includes writing down all the tasks your team needs to do and crossing off each one as it is completed. That makes it easier to remember what you need to do when you're getting tired during the late-night hours of a hackathon. It also helps you keep track of your schedule. If you start to fall behind, you can drop less important tasks.
2. Do one thing at a time. Hackathon team members should focus their energies on completing one task at a time. But it's also important to avoid spending too much time on any one task or product feature. Time limits should be set for every task. You might find that some later tasks don't take as long as you think, and that you can come back to earlier challenging tasks.
3. Clearly present your idea. Being able to do this is crucial. The peers to whom you're presenting at an internal company hackathon need to understand both

your idea and the benefits it will provide. Without that, you won't get their support to pursue it further.

Kozma explains, "You can create the coolest thing in the world; however, if you don't explain the benefits in a way that your audience understands, it won't matter."

Early hackathon ideas that ultimately became successful include a tool that lets customers download Shutterstock video clips in any file format, and another that translates the site into forty different languages.[85] The "Suggested Images" feature on Shutterstock's site also had its genesis during a hackathon.[86] All these ideas helped to create the type of user experience that gives Shutterstock a competitive advantage.

One brilliant hackathon idea was Spectrum, a tool that allows Shutterstock users to search its photo library using color. This search tool is perfect for designers who may not be able to articulate exactly what they are looking for using keywords, but who need to make use of color to create compelling designs. It has proved very popular since it was launched in March 2013.

Shutterstock staff ideas also led to the development of Offset, an important start-up business within the company. Offset was launched in 2013 and provides high-end, artistic imagery that serves a target segment outside of Shutterstock's core market. After identifying this opportunity, Shutterstock assembled an internal team of product developers, designers, and engineers to make this product offering a reality. It provides premium-quality images for billboards, book covers, and signage, and for the customer, it's quite a bit cheaper than organizing a photo shoot and hiring talent.

Offset images are captured by award-winning artists, and they are significantly more expensive than Shutterstock images. Offset deliberately created a premium marketplace for high-end photographers. Unlike the standard Shutterstock marketplace where any person can apply to submit their photos for display and potential user download, Offset only accepts photos from a handpicked list of photographers. That helps Offset maintain its premium quality differentiation.

Offset developed as a start-up with the full backing and support of Shutterstock, broadening the company's range of products and its market appeal.

In 2014, the year after the release of the Spectrum tool and the launch of Offset, the company's revenue increased by thirty-nine percent on the previous year.[87]

There have been other hackathon success stories since — like Sequence, an easy-to-use in-browser video editor developed for Shutterstock's website. This innovation won the overall hackathon prize when it was first whiteboarded. The company subsequently gave the staff who came up with the idea time to fully develop it, and the Sequence product was created. It allows users to conveniently search and edit video files within Shutterstock's huge collection, without needing to upload them into a different program. Many users like to mix Shutterstock video with their own footage to create exactly what they want. Sequence allows them to experiment with different Shutterstock clips before making their purchase decisions.

Today, Shutterstock has more than 169 million royalty-free images, video clips, and music tracks available for download, and an annual revenue of $494.3 million.[88] Its success can be attributed to a large extent to the culture it has created that encourages staff innovation and creativity.

Strategies for creating distance from your plans

If you want to create the kind of workplace where creativity and innovation can happen quickly, and not after twenty hours of planning meetings, try these exercises.

Develop a kill list

Stop for a minute and think about how many planning meetings you had in the last year. Think about every single one. The internal meetings, the huddles, the touch-bases, the check-ins, the come-by-my-desks, the operations meetings, the team meetings, and meetings about the other kinds of meetings you should have had.

Now, do your best to kill as many of those meetings as possible. If you were responsible for calling some of them, killing those ones should be easy. You're probably part of the problem for your team!

Explain to your team why you're killing the number of meetings. The goal is to liberate them and give them the time to do what they do best: think and create ideas, rather than talking about them *ad nauseam*. Invite team members to scrutinize their own internal meetings and ditch any that can be replaced with action.

For the other meetings on your kill list that someone else in your organization regularly calls, think about whether you or your team really need to attend. Are you just going out of habit or to be polite? If you are, stop going. Or at least go less regularly. Read the meeting minutes afterward instead and take any necessary action then.

You can also try and tactfully suggest how those meetings could be more productive for you and your team. You'll probably find that others in your organization feel the same way.

Split meeting time into planning and doing

If you want to squeeze more productivity from every meeting, try this: Allot half of your meeting time to planning and the other half to doing small tasks that team members can knock off before they leave the meeting room.

The planning half: Quickly start the meeting by briefing team members on the project and assigning tasks and deadlines to each person. If it's a progress meeting, get each team member to provide an update on the specific tasks they completed since the last meeting. Providing regular progress updates will kick the procrastination habit — individuals will have to work at a steady pace if they want to avoid disappointing (or irritating) their teammates.

The doing half: Many people can sense the end of a meeting as it nears. They'll gather their belongings and scoot to the edge of their seats. Their minds have already switched from the present meeting to the next tasks that need their attention. When they get around to working on your project again, they'll ask themselves, "What did I commit to doing, again?" They'll need to spend extra time reviewing meeting notes and refreshing their memories.

Don't let team members leave the meeting room once the progress updates are complete. Use the remaining meeting time to tackle the next set of tasks. Team members who need to meet in smaller groups can do so; people who need to phone clients or vendors can do so; people who need to source products can do so. It's amazing what you can get done in fifteen minutes when everyone is completely focused on one project.

Introduce a company hackathon

While hackathons trace their origins to the computer programming industry, many creative organizations are now using the model so participants can create a viable concept within twenty-four hours. If you're going to hold a hackathon at your organization, laser-like focus and incentives are key to success. Follow these tips:

- Be positive and welcoming. Focus on building a sense of community — everyone is coming together through their shared loved of creativity and trying new things. Invite everyone to participate and give them the opportunity learn something new.

- Choose good projects. According to hackathon guru Joshua Tauberer, projects that make good candidates for hackathon are those that are clearly articulated, have attainable goals, are easy for newcomers to jump on, are led by a stakeholder, and are organized.[89] Projects that are too complex or diffuse won't set teams up for success.
- Cover the venue essentials. You'll need a space with good seating, a power strip at each table, reliable Wi-Fi, a projector, a microphone, and bathrooms. Bring in healthy food and drinks that will keep people feeling positive and energized. Avoid pizza and heavy food.
- Encourage diverse teams. Let participants create their own teams, but take a page from Shutterstock's book and require teams to represent a variety of people and departments. Get every team to assign a project leader and a timekeeper.
- Share, celebrate, and reward. At the end of the hackathon session, get each team to make a two-minute presentation outlining what they worked on, achieved, and learned. Host a short wrap-up party to celebrate everyone's contributions. Reward top projects with prizes and swag.

Following the hackathon, choose the best ideas and develop them further during regular work hours.

Incorporate some "Zen Habits" into your life

Leo Babauta writes the *Zen Habits* blog, which has twice been named one of the top twenty-five blogs by *Time* magazine. We admire Babauta because he has uncopyrighted his entire body of work, and he doesn't believe in limiting distribution to protect profits.

The follow tips were adapted from Babauta's "Ten Steps to Take Action and Eliminate Bureaucracy" blog post.[90]

Eliminate paperwork wherever possible:
Paperwork (even if it's in electronic form) is necessary for many things. But you'll often find that a lot of organizational paperwork is unnecessary and that it slows the creativity of you and your team down. Evaluate what paperwork you do and don't need for your creative projects, and make sure that any forms are streamlined.

Cut out unnecessary processes:
If there are steps or approval processes that are slowing you or your creative team down, can they be eliminated or at least reduced? Processes often become routines in organizations that outlive their usefulness over time.

Empower your staff:
If you're leading a team of creatives, don't be a decision-making bottleneck. If you've hired or chosen good people for your team, give them the freedom to do what they do best. Give them clear guidelines, but allow them to work independently as much as you can.

Hire and work with action-oriented people:
When you're recruiting your creative team, look for people with a track record of getting things done. Give them a trial and see if they tend to focus on actions and decision, or processes and paperwork. Hire and reward action-oriented people. This habit will reinforce that action is your priority.

7.

INVERT THE
ORG CHART

Place the innovation responsibility where it can
thrive — with the people who are free to fail.

Organizations put structures and systems in place to manage the
outcomes and outputs of their staff and teams. They document
their structure in an organizational chart. While these structures
bring clarity for organizations, they often trump innovation.

Early in my career, I was hired by one of the most respected
advertising agencies in the city. I was thrilled to join their ranks,
get the business card, and add the agency's name to my LinkedIn
profile.

This agency was very traditional in its organization structure
at the time. You had the creative director (CD) at the top of the
creative department, followed by the associate creative director
(ACD) and director of creative services (D of CS). Next came the
studio art directors, then the graphic designers and copywriters.

When a client would sign off on a creative brief, the account
rep would come down to the creative department and meet with
the D of CS. The director would look at the budget and the need,
and then assign people and hours to the project.

The account rep would then go to the CD and ACD and present the brief. They would discuss it, and then call me and a graphic designer into the office. The account rep would present the brief again, and then the CD and ACD would provide instructions for the type of concept they wanted us to produce for the ad campaign.

Next, the designer and I would meet separately and get three concepts down on paper. We would go back to the CD and ACD to present our three ideas. If we had done a good job, they would approve one concept and then advise us how to write the copy and execute the design. We'd head back to our desks to prepare proofs of the ad concept for the client's review.

On Friday afternoons, there would be a line of creative team members standing outside the creative director's office. We'd have printouts of ad proofs in our hands, each with a slug at the bottom of the document with three signature lines: one for the D of CS, one for the ACD, and one for the CD. It was not until those three signatures were in place that the ad proofs could leave the agency.

This corporate structure was one of the things that gave the agency its credibility. Three very experienced advertising professionals had to sign off on every single piece, so that clients never received sloppy creative work.

Sticking to the organizational structure also meant the agency's offering remained traditional during the years I worked there. It was the place to go for billboard, radio, TV, and print campaigns because that's what the three people at the top of the creative department knew best, and those three people directed the concept for every piece of advertising that came through the shop.

Clients that wanted the latest digital or experiential advertising campaigns would leave or add additional agency partners to their rosters. Creative professionals who wanted to try their hands at new and emerging advertising techniques would also have to leave.

Few businesses have the luxury to focus on their strengths and ignore everything else. For many companies, losing talent and client confidence will eventually bankrupt you. When evaluating whether your company is built to evolve, be sure to look at your org chart.

Where does innovation live in your company?

Redesigning the organizational structure to meet the demands of fast-changing workforces and industries is a top concern of business leaders. Only eight percent of organizations believe their current structure is optimized, and only four percent have no plans to fix them.[91]

The traditional org chart has a pyramid shape, with a few leaders at the top and many worker bees at the bottom. It's often people at the top of the chart who are expected to lead the company into new eras of innovation and success. The Proximity Paradox of the traditional org chart is that this group is in the worst position to innovate.

Senior leaders face the highest expectations for company performance, and therefore have the least freedom to take the risks and make the mistakes required for innovation. The company ultimately succeeds or fails under their guidance. Since they guide big decisions, their mistakes can be very costly and are often grounds for dismissal.

That pressure can trigger a stress response that inhibits their creativity. Psychologist Daniel Goleman, who wrote the bestselling book, *Emotional Intelligence*, coined the term "amygdala hijack" — a process where fear or stress triggers the amygdala neurons to block our other brain systems. These neurons tell the body to fight, flight, or freeze for self-defense.[92] Counseling psychologist Dr. Jena Field later explored how the concept affects creativity. She says creative work requires us to take risks, and the fear of failure or embarrassment can shut down the parts of the brain needed for creativity.[93]

The people at the bottom of the org chart are often only responsible for their tasks — not the results of the company. Failure incurs a talking to or a slap on the wrist. These are the people who have the cognitive freedom to think creatively and take risks, and yet they often are not given the opportunity to do so.

Fig 2: The traditional organizational chart, where ↑ represents freedom to innovate and ⇩ represents the pressure to produce results for the company.

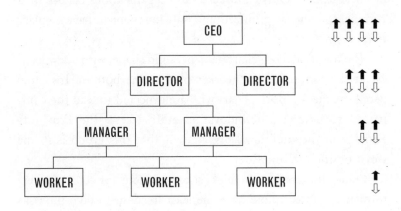

We need to create opportunities where it's safe for the organization's leaders to hand their innovation freedom to someone who doesn't carry the same burden to produce results. The organizational chart helps us create distance between the people responsible for success and the people with the freedom to fail.

Can you defer to authority and challenge the status quo?

Society encourages the deference to authority on which organizational charts rely. Children are generally brought up to obey parents who are following the child-rearing traditions that have been passed down, consciously or unconsciously, for generations. At college, students will write the essay that will earn an A grade from the professor and get them a spot on the Dean's List. A professional cellist will follow the cues of the conductor and perform the piece of music selected by the music director to stay in good standing with the orchestra.

In an organization, staff will produce work that fulfills the expectations of their manager and moves the company closer to the goals set out by the CEO.

Deference to authority engages your rational brain. *What do I need to do to get approval from the boss?* You think of all the past projects that were approved, examine what made them successful, and then apply the same formula to your current project. But this cycle fosters the homogenous thinking that breeds complacency and kills creativity.

Innovation requires someone to challenge the status quo. You need to speak up, ruffle a few feathers, and say to the boss, "Trust me on this one." When you're creating something new, there is always a period of thrashing, where you must temporarily defy authority and cause some discomfort to co-workers while you bring form to your idea.

It often isn't until your invention is on the home stretch that others will see its value. And if you're working in an organization that values performance or efficiency over innovation, you may get reprimanded before you hit that home stretch.

It's counter to human nature to push back against authority, and the people who seem to have a knack for rebelling typically aren't embraced in the average workplace.

To make the window for innovation even narrower, people higher up the org chart often feel they should have answers for their direct reports — not more problems to solve. Saying, "I don't know what we should do" when a challenge arises suggests a lack of confidence and acumen. Like we discussed in Chapter Two, managers may naturally fall back to their old solutions when their reports come looking for guidance on new problems.

Without staff who regularly challenge the status quo and put their necks on the line, and without bosses who can say, "I don't have the answer; what do you think we should do?", innovation will continue to start and end with the senior leadership team.

A good org chart needs to put the innovative people within your company on equal footing with the authority figures. If leadership appears to hold all the power and call all the shots, even the most creative thinkers will fall into line.

Rethink your organizational chart in a way that allows for creativity. Ultimately, innovation should drive what gets done — not the other way around.

The organizational chart that makes the world's most advanced textiles

W.L. Gore & Associates (or Gore, for short) is a multinational manufacturer headquartered in Delaware. It has about 9,500 staff spread across more than twenty-five countries around the world. Its most well-known product is Gore-Tex. This is a lightweight, waterproof fabric used in clothing (for people like hikers, astronauts, and soldiers) and medical implants (for things like heart patches and synthetic blood vessels), as well as in a wide range of industrial and electronics products.[94]

Innovation is key to the company's success. It has helped it to survive and thrive in a dynamic industry that is subject to IT developments, globalization, intense competition, and the inevitable ups and downs of economic cycles.

One way that Gore & Associates promotes innovation is via its unique organizational structure, which can be traced back to the company's founder, the late Bill Gore. Terri Kelly, President and CEO of W.L. Gore & Associates, said that he "hated policy manuals and bureaucratic ways of telling the organization what to do."[95] Those types of traditional organizational structures were even more common in the early days of the company's existence in the 1960s than they are today, so Bill Gore was certainly a visionary in his outlook.

Bill Gore was in his mid-forties when he founded the company in 1958 using his life savings. Previously, he had worked at another large multinational (DuPont) for his entire career. There he had seen firsthand how innovation can be stifled in a large, bureaucratic organization. He knew that innovation was going to be crucial to his new, technology-driven venture. He wanted to create a company with no fixed hierarchical structure, where all staff would be free to be creative and talk to anyone else.

Bill Gore created a "lattice" organizational structure for his new venture, where all staff were connected to each other. There were no layers of management like you'd find in a traditional structure. He wanted to empower his self-managed teams to make decisions, solve problems, and come up with innovative ideas.

He explained the structure and how it facilitates innovative actions:

> A lattice organization is one that involves direct transactions, self-commitment, [and] natural leadership, and lacks assigned or assumed authority . . . Every successful organization has a lattice organization that underlies the facade of authoritarian hierarchy. It is through these lattice organizations that things get done, and most of us delight in going around the formal procedures and doing things the straightforward and easy way.[96]

This approach is relatively easy to implement in a small organization, but harder to maintain as it grows. However, the Gore company has managed to largely maintain it as the organization has grown, and for good reason. It has reaped substantial benefits along the way.

Over time, the founding structure has evolved to now include some elements of a traditional organizational structure, such as product-focused business units with their own leaders. But the underlying philosophy of having flat (or minimal) layers of management is still alive today at Gore plants all over the world.

You won't find job titles like supervisors, managers, and vice presidents at Gore. Self-managed teams remain the fundamental building blocks of the organization's structure. These teams negotiate the job roles of their members as is necessary for the project they're working on.

Staff are rewarded with ten percent "dabble time," where they can explore new project ideas that they are passionate about. They are empowered to experiment and not punished for failing in their attempts to develop innovative ideas.

Ideas are peer reviewed and team leaders emerge from this experimentation process. Those who can create a vision for their innovative idea and inspire others to follow them get the opportunity to create a new team and develop their product idea. The company views this as natural leadership, rather than the traditional organizational structure approach of appointing bosses.

In this way, Gore's organizational structure is continuously evolving over time to focus on new ideas. Staff also get to work on projects that interest them. This increases their level of commitment to the innovation projects and the success of the organization.

The teams evaluate the dabble time ideas using three criteria:

- **Real:** Is the opportunity real? In other words, would there be a market for it?
- **Win:** Could Gore win in that market?
- **Worth:** Is the idea so unique and valuable that the company

could make money from it? Does the idea have the potential to create a sustainable competitive advantage for Gore?

The company believes strongly in the power of small teams. Authority is delegated to these teams. They discourage plants of more than 250 workers.[97] Bill Gore once famously remarked: "Once a unit reaches a certain size, 'we decided' becomes 'they decided.'" The company also believes that larger plants have the potential to inhibit staff communication.

Existing team members are actively involved in the interviewing and recruitment process for new staff. When hired, each new staff member is assigned a mentor (called a sponsor) to help him or her develop and succeed at the company.

Individuals and teams can communicate directly with anyone in the organization to get what they need to be successful. The Gore company encourages cross-functional collaboration by having R&D specialists, staff, engineers, salespeople, chemists, and machinists working in the same plant. This goes against the traditional approach of having specialist plants and offices for different functions to create efficiencies. The company believes that the collaborative benefits of their structural approach far outweighs the costs.

Staff at Gore (who are called "associates" to reflect both the company's name and its philosophy) are compensated according to their peer-reviewed contributions to their team. They are also provided with shares in the company, so that they have buy-in to its successes and failures. Team members are accountable to their team, rather than to bosses.

Gore is an extremely innovative company, as demonstrated by the more than 2,000 worldwide patents it has been granted in its near sixty-year history. Its patents span a wide range of fields, including electronics, medical devices, and polymer processing. Its current annual revenue exceeds US$3 billion.[98]

Its record of successfully introducing new products into diverse markets speaks for itself. The company has no fear of attacking new markets. One well-known example is the plastic coating it developed to create Elixir acoustic guitar strings. These strings last three to five times longer than normal guitar strings and quickly became the market leader in an industry that hadn't had a technical breakthrough in decades. Another is Glide dental floss, which allows people to floss smaller gaps between their teeth more easily.[99] These were entirely new markets for the company that its innovative products helped it conquer.

And not only is the company financially successful, it's frequently cited in various surveys as being one of the best and most innovative companies to work for at its various locations all around the world.

Success stories like these are a testament to the company's organizational structure. Innovative ideas have continued to emerge as it has grown from a small fledgling operation in Delaware into a multinational conglomerate. That's because it has retained the underlying philosophy of its original structure.

It hasn't morphed into the traditional management pyramid that characterizes the organizational structure of many larger organizations. That structure stifles creativity. The company is organized to promote innovation. It isn't relying on centralized managers to make its key decisions. Instead, authority in its flat organizational structure is pushed out to operating teams that are empowered and motivated to succeed. And that's how innovative ideas flourish within Gore.

The current CEO of Gore is Terri Kelly. She began her career with the company as a process engineer in 1983. In the company's typical style, she was appointed CEO following a peer-driven selection process. She explains what it's like to lead a non-hierarchical organizational structure.

I think, as it looks in practice, it's pretty dynamic, where we organize more around opportunity. It's pretty fluid, versus a static organization. I think the leadership moves based on what problem is being solved. So, I think in traditional companies, it's a pretty fixed hierarchy of who the leaders are and who they report to, where it's maybe a little bit more difficult to see that in our organization because we purposely try to make it more dynamic.

She also explains how the company's innovation culture is maintained:

We have what we call rainmakers and implementers. Rainmakers come up with wild ideas, implementers make them real. The two drive each other crazy. If you're not careful, control will gravitate to the implementers. So, we try to protect the rainmakers. That means we have to be comfortable with more chaos. Our organization is used to dealing with chaos; we have a high tolerance for it. We like to respond to crises. When the ship is under attack, the level of ownership is high, culturally.[100]

Strategies for creating distance from org chart responsibilities

If the Gore story makes you say, "I wish we could do that," then it's time to reassign innovation responsibilities within your company. Let innovation drive your structure and what gets done — not the other way around. Here are two ways you can do that.

Invert the innovation responsibility

Encourage innovation from the ground up in your organization. Create an environment where people feel comfortable putting ideas forward, providing different perspectives, and challenging the status quo. Staff who are closest to the action will have the easiest time seeing new problems to solve or opportunities to seize.

Here are a few things to consider when flipping the org chart and adopting a Gore-style approach to innovation.

1. Add innovation to your frontline workers' job descriptions. Update the job descriptions for current employees, explain the new expectations, and create a monthly forum where staff can meet off-site to discuss new ideas.

2. Set a framework for evaluating new ideas. Look to the company's vision statement or strategic plan when selecting criteria, rather than appointing a senior leader to arbitrarily evaluate ideas. Successful ideas should align with the company's financial, cultural, and social responsibility goals.

3. Give successful ideas a budget and a team. Decide on the amount of money and employee hours you are willing to invest in developing the best ideas. If your frontline workers are currently at max capacity, it may mean hiring additional staff to free up the dabble time staff need to execute their ideas.

4. Make sure senior leaders buy in. If your frontline workers (who are in the best position to innovate) have found an idea that meets the selection criteria, and they are willing to invest time in it, leadership's job is to now mentor and support the group of employees

tasked with bringing the idea to life — not to
stonewall the idea or remold it.

Fig. 3: The traditional organization with the responsibility for creativity flipped,
where ↑ represents freedom to innovate and ⇩ represents the pressure to
produce results for the company.

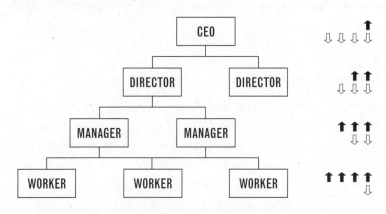

Make note of the ideas with which you disagree

Take a moment to reflect back on ideas that your team has presented
to you in the last six months. You may not be able to remember all
of them, but when you've got a few minutes, jot down as many as
you can. Indicate which of the ideas were brought to life. Note the
percentage that you approved and the percentage that you didn't.
Of the ideas you approved, how many fit with your existing ideals
and values? How many did you approve even though you did not
agree with them?

Typically, through this exercise, managers notice that they only
approve ideas that line up with their own beliefs. If they do not
see the relevance of the idea or agree with it, they do not give it
the green light.

If you're that kind of manager, we encourage you to challenge
your assumptions. The next time the team brings forward ideas for

consideration, approve one that does not line up with your existing beliefs. Force yourself to argue why the idea they proposed *could* work, and then pitch the idea back to the team to ensure you currently understand their thinking.

Even if the idea fails down the line, you'll signal to your team that you are open to divergent thinking and are willing to see beyond your own biases. You may also find those biases loosen up over time.

Be honest and open about your own innovation bias

None of us want to admit that we are resistant to change and new ideas — we feel it is a weakness.

If you can be open with yourself and your team about where your innovation biases lie, you'll become more open to accepting new ideas. Try this: reveal your biases to your team. Invite team members to challenge your biases when they crop up at work. If you own the fact that you prefer the color blue, and someone pitches red, you can talk about it. You may eventually see the merits of red.

Challenge org chart assumptions

Sometimes we don't need to make any changes to our org chart or how our teams interact. Sometimes all we need to do is refuse to accept cop-outs for ourselves, our leaders, and our subordinates.

If you talk to a random employee at a random organization, there is a good chance they'll say that it's not their place to come up with new ideas or to challenge the status quo. If you talk to that employee's CEO, they'll call bullshit. They'll tell you they would *love* it if a frontline employee came forward with an innovative, new idea.

As frontline employees, sometimes all we need to do is take a risk, champion an idea, go right to the top, and pitch the hell out of our concept. We need to be direct in our communication and go directly to the chief decision-maker.

Clear middle-management roadblocks

If you report to middle-management, there is a good chance you have a hard time pushing creative or innovative ideas past organizational roadblocks. Middle managers face pressure from both sides: the bottom of the organization and the top of the organization.

As a frontline employee, recognize this pressure when you approach a mid-level manager with a new idea. Before proposing an idea, identify ways that your manager might feel a sense of ownership over it. Egos can be fragile; there is a good chance your mid-level manager does not feel like they are being creative or innovative enough themselves. An idea from a subordinate can feel a bit threatening. Be conscious of this dynamic — find a way that you and your manager can jointly own the idea or partner on bringing it to life. You might find the roadblocks disappear.

PART THREE:

DISTANCE FROM INDUSTRY

When we think about the future, we hope for a future of progress. That progress can take one of two forms. Horizontal or extensive progress means copying things that work — going from one to n. Horizontal progress is easy to imagine because we already know what it looks like. Vertical or intensive progress means doing new things — going from zero to one. Vertical progress is harder to imagine because it requires doing something nobody else has ever done. If you take one typewriter and build 100, you have made horizontal progress. If you have a typewriter and build a word processor, you have made vertical progress.

— Peter Thiel, *Zero to One*

Our culture celebrates the people and companies that bring bold change to their industry — advertising campaigns that don't shy away from the social reform their industry needs; apps that transform the way customers access an old-fashioned service;

entrepreneurs who bootstrap a product that our world never even knew it needed. But how do you bring this kind of bold progress (or "vertical progress," as Peter Thiel would say) to your organization? The first step is to shake off the Proximity Paradox that leads you to believe you're operating within a box of constraints.

When I was ten years old, I loved learning about animals and how they lived. I would visit the library and check out all the titles on the history and care of different animals. I had a pet hamster named Dolly, and I once spent an hour and a half reciting hamster history to my sister's friend. It's not how most ten-year-olds would choose to spend their afternoon. And, I am quite sure it's not what my sister's friend had planned.

One day, I discovered a book on hamster husbandry and learned that hamsters have one of the shortest gestation periods of all mammals (eighteen days). I had been looking for a way to make money from my home, and I knew that lots of kids at school were buying small pets. So I bought a male hamster to breed with Dolly.

The first male was a dud. He wasn't interested in breeding, so I returned him to the pet store. It was an odd reason for a kid to return a hamster, but the pet store allowed me to exchange him for a different male.

The next male was on his game. Soon, I had a litter of baby hamsters. I sold them to my friends at a discounted price of $5, but after a few litters, I had a surplus. I called a national chain of pet stores and asked to speak to the manager. As a kid, I didn't really know how one was supposed to sell hamsters to a pet store, but I figured there was no harm in asking. The manager on the other end of the line was surprised to hear a ten-year-old kid asking about his hamster-procurement process. Many of the national chains buy from large wholesale suppliers through a traditional tender process, but this particular manager found that process to be tedious. He was open to a more nimble idea.

I told him I had some hamsters to sell and said I could regularly supply them — not a lot of volume, but a regular stream of beauties. He agreed to give me a shot.

Black hamsters were quite rare in pet stores, so that's where I started. I tried to get orange and black combos, as they are more rare still. I didn't have a ton of luck in this department as it turns out that only females could be this color due to recessive and dominant genes, or something along those lines. Nonetheless, I was able to sell my little critters.

My hamster-breeding business only lasted a couple of years. Eventually, having a bunch of hamsters in my house became more work than it was worth. I made about $500, which may not seem like a lot, but the profit margins were pretty good for a ten-year-old kid's business.

I realize the scale of my operation was pretty miniscule compared to what was happening with national suppliers, but a well-connected network of kid businesses could potentially shake up the market from a very unexpected place. As a child, I could see this opportunity because I was free from expectations to fit into a pet store's traditional hamster-procurement model.

Your company may feel like a box of constraints, thickly padded with rules on what you can and cannot do with your brand, products, and marketing. It's often no better outside the walls of your office. Your industry is simply a larger box with its own code of accepted activities and behaviors. To truly break free from your competition, you need to create distance from your industry.

In this section, we'll show you how to escape the box and find new customers to serve and new companies to compete with.

8.

CREATE FOR
FUTURE CUSTOMERS

Current customers are complacent; make big changes to attract the next loyal following.

Do you ever feel like the more you focus on keeping your existing customers happy, the more you feel constrained by their needs?

Age-old marketing principles tell us to reward loyal customers and use them as ambassadors for our brand. They also tell us it's cheaper to retain an existing customer than to attract a new one. Often an unsatisfied customer can be retained with a personal gesture, such as a phone call or a small gift, while new customers require a long courting process before they can be convinced to switch to your product or service.

But the downside of a customer retention mindset is that it undermines your ability to innovate and create new products and services, because you're focused on what your customers currently want versus what they might actually need.

Think about how mad your parents got when they had to replace their first smartphone with a new model, or how upset you get when Facebook changes its interface. If given the choice, your parents would likely stick with their old phones and you'd likely keep using the old Facebook interface, because you're both comfortable with them. Your current customers often think the same way.

If Facebook never updated its features and interface because it was afraid of pissing off current customers, it would never have grown to be the largest social media platform in the world.[101]

The people who fell in love with your brand last year are likely not the same people who are going to make you more successful next year.

Many small tokens versus a few grand gestures

Picture a sprawling agricultural trade show in the middle of January. The heating system is working overtime to fend off the bitter cold, and inside, thousands of people in boots and ball caps sweat under their winter coats. The sand footing from the cattle and horse competition arenas has been scraped away, and now hundreds of trade-show booths crowd together in narrow rows.

Here, you can buy everything from a $4 tub of farm-fresh honey to a million-dollar tractor. There are snake-oil traders hocking miracle treatments for sore joints, livestock breeders hocking bookings for their prize bull, grain buyers hocking their low-risk-high-reward sales contracts, and seed companies hocking their newest variety of wheat.

Everyone has a something to give to visitors who stop by their trade-show booth. Advertising agencies can get rich quick by producing materials for the businesses that attend these shows. The client request will often look like this:

"We want a trade show strategy. Our goal is to get 100 new customers, which equates to $1 million in sales. We have a budget of $250,000 to produce branded giveaways. We expect 50,000 people to come by the booth, so we need 50,000 pieces."

This type of request has always confused me. I've attended the trade shows, and after one day of walking the floor and visiting the booths, you could fill the bed of a truck with stress balls, mini-flashlight key chains, iPhone attachments, pens and notebooks, along with gloves, hats, and T-shirts.

No one's tchotchkes stand out from the rest, yet every business feels they must produce them. They're afraid that if a loyal customer comes by the booth, and their trade-show staff do not have a branded hat to offer them, that customer will be offended and take their business elsewhere.

Every company says their trade-show goal is to acquire new customers. Yet if you asked the marketing manager at the agriculture company, "Can you identify 100 farmers whom you would love to acquire as customers," they would say, "Yes."

And then if you asked, "Do you know what those 100 farmers want from your company," they would again say, "Yes."

Finally, if you asked, "Why not take your $250,000 and use it to do something really special for those 100 farmers when they're in town for the trade show," they would say, "We can't because we would have nothing left to spend on small gifts for our existing customers."

I've never understood the logic. I find it hard to believe that a loyal customer would walk away from their favorite brand if they didn't get a laser pen from a trade-show booth. But a customer is often worth a minimum of $10,000 to a seed company, so it's an expensive risk to take. Therefore, companies continue to spend hundreds of thousands of dollars a year on tchotchkes to mitigate that risk. At the same time, they abandon the opportunity to get new customers.

Innovation doesn't come from places of comfort and security

Why do we set big goals but then hesitate to make the correspondingly big changes required to achieve them? With product innovation, we often opt for small, incremental product improvements. In marketing, we might split the budget so that half of the funds are spent rewarding existing customers and half are allocated to a new customer-acquisition strategy.

Organizational leadership may say, "We want our customers to grow with our product." What they're really saying is, "We need to get better so we can attract new customers, but we don't want to freak out our existing customers to the point that they leave."

In other words, companies want to have their cake and eat it, too. But innovation doesn't come from places of comfort and security.

Branding expert Kevin Roberts says great ideas come from the fringes — from the places where resources are scarce, and you have nothing to lose and everything to gain.[102] The people on the fringes (like disruptive start-ups) don't have loyal customers to offend. Their outsider position creates the distance necessary to fully explore the needs of an ideal customer. Their mindset is fully geared to acquisition.

If you have a retention mindset, you'll wrestle with the Proximity Paradox. Rewarding loyal customers will become your MO. You'll focus your attention on customer satisfaction surveys and net-promoter scores — items that show how your customers felt in past. This data cannot guarantee future performance, and worse yet, it keeps your attention on old actions. You'll fail to see the new idea and opportunities on the fringes.

Is your product ten times better than the one a prospect is currently using?

> Many entrepreneurs fall into the trap of building products that are only marginally better than existing solutions, hoping their innovation will be good enough to woo customers away from existing products.[103]
>
> — Nir Eyal, *Hooked*

According to internet pioneer Bill Gross, you must be ten times better than your competition to get a potential customer to switch. If you want a competitor's customer to step out of the comfort zone afforded by their current product choice, and willingly wrestle with the learning curve required to learn yours, your product must be irresistibly better to make it worth their while.

Consider this sobering statistic. John T. Gourville, a professor at Harvard Business School, says 30,000 new packaged goods are introduced to the US food industry every year. Only ten percent to thirty percent will survive on store shelves for more than twelve months.

Gourville goes on to say, "Consumers overvalue the existing benefits of an entrenched product by a factor of three, while developers overvalue the new benefits of their innovation by a factor of three. The result is a mismatch of nine to one, or nine times, between what innovators think consumers desire and what consumers really want."[104]

Is your product nine or ten times better than the competition's? If not, what will it take to get there? To make that size of change, you'll need to temporarily put the needs of loyal customers on the back burner. It will be uncomfortable, and a few existing customers may jump ship along the way, but freeing yourself to pursue new customers will invite a new level of innovation and creativity into your organization.

When the hard-core gamer market was saturated, Nintendo found a new, untapped audience

You probably don't realize it, but multinational Japanese consumer electronics and video game company Nintendo began as a manufacturer of handmade playing cards! That was way back in 1889, but Nintendo continued with that product focus for the next six decades. No one could have imagined the high-tech video game industry that Nintendo would eventually dominate.

The company has adapted and evolved over time. One of the reasons it has been able to both survive and thrive at different times in its long history is by continually innovating to attract new customers. This mindset was perfectly demonstrated by how it reacted when the hard-core video gaming market became saturated.

Nintendo entered the video game industry in 1974. In the early 1980s, it released its first major success: the iconic *Donkey Kong* game that introduced the now-famous Mario character. The video game industry exploded over the subsequent decades and Nintendo rode the wave. They subsequently developed a video game franchise around Mario and other popular games they developed, including Pokémon.

With the surging popularity of video games, the industry became highly competitive and saturated with a seemingly endless array of products. Advances in technology also meant that high-quality video games can be produced and distributed online by smaller start-ups.

In addition to Nintendo, dominant players that emerged in the video game industry include other multinational giants, such as Electronic Arts, Sony, Microsoft, and Sega. It became increasingly difficult for the established companies to grow their already large revenues in the face of intense and increasing competition.

The Japanese economy also experienced a prolonged period of recession in the 1990s and early 2000s when the market was reaching maturity. Nintendo's then-president Hiroshu Yamauchi remarked at the time, "If we can increase the scope of the industry, we can re-energize the global market and lift Japan out of depression — that is Nintendo's mission."[105]

Nintendo realized that the best way to increase sales in the crowded and mature video game market was to try and attract new video game users with a revolutionary new product. By significantly differentiating their offering, they could potentially attract people that had previously never bothered with video games. That differentiation and the innovation it required became their primary focus.

The alternative — just making incremental improvements to their existing video game consoles and games — wouldn't deliver consistent and long-term growth any longer. A retention mindset and preaching to the converted just wouldn't cut it.

Nintendo already had products that would appeal to their existing video game users. But a revolutionary new product might encourage gamers who were using competitor products to switch to them. Focusing on new markets was unlikely to hurt them, and there was enormous potential upside.

Nintendo spent the early years of the 21st century focusing on developing the innovative new products they needed. In late 2006, they released the Nintendo Wii, a revolutionary new console that was designed to be more inclusive than hard-core gaming products like the Sony PlayStation and Microsoft's Xbox 360 (which both were targeted at existing video gamers).

The Wii had a broader potential appeal than traditional video games. Instead of pressing buttons on a controller to swing a racket, steer a car, or do whatever action you need to do, the Wii allowed users to physically mimic the action. The Wii had a slim wand that wirelessly connected to its console. The wand contained motion sensors that detected three-dimensional movements. Rather than being stuck at a console, the Wii allowed users to move around and perform the actions they needed, and those actions would be mimicked on the screen.

Wii revolutionized the user experience and made it possible for more people to take part in video games. For example, instead of having to know which button to press to hit a ball in a tennis game, you just mimicked the action intuitively. This meant that the

Wii was suitable for both video game novices as well as hard-core gamers. Suddenly, Wii made video games potentially accessible for everyone — people of all ages, male and female, whether they had ever used video games before or not.

At the time of the Wii's launch, Nintendo America's COO, Reggie Fils-Aimé, said:

> Our visuals for Wii look fantastic, but in the end, prettier pictures will not bring new gamers and casual gamers into this industry. It has to be about the ability to pick up a controller, not be intimidated, and have fun immediately. The trick is being able to do that, not only with the new casual gamer, but do it in a way that the core gamer gets excited as well.[106]

The Wii's ease of use certainly opened new markets for Nintendo. It allowed the company to capitalize on a significant demographic trend — the aging population in many countries around the world. For example, in the US, the Wii helped the over-sixty segment to become the fastest growing in the video game market.[107] Nintendo strategically placed Wii consoles in retirement villages and other senior citizen venues and created a range of appealing games for this new audience, like simulated bowling, golf, and tennis tournaments.

A focus on sporting games also helped to encourage other first-time video gamers to use the Wii. Most people already knew the rules of popular sports and how to play them. They didn't have to go through the common video game experience of learning how to play a new game.

Fitness was another favorable demographic trend that Wii exploited to capture new markets. In 2007, it developed the Wii Fit, containing a wireless balance board with multiple pressure sensors. These sensors allowed the user to physically mimic actions when doing exercise games, including aerobics, strength training, and yoga. The Wii Fit console was adopted in nursing homes, physio-therapy clinics, and fitness centers.

Nintendo actively encouraged third-party developers to create as many games as possible for their new and growing market segments, by ensuring that the development costs for Wii games were low. Developers could create games for the Wii at a fraction of the cost of traditional games, giving Nintendo a major competitive advantage.

Graphics and sound are typically very costly to develop for video games. But Nintendo deliberately kept the Wii's graphics and sounds less sophisticated, because the focus was on the ease and physical experience of playing a game on the device. And the more games that are available for a device, the more likely it is for consumers to buy it over a competing product.

The focus on the user experience was a major point of difference for the Wii. When video games from Electronic Arts and Rockstar Games were trying to differentiate based on their graphics, Wii games differentiated through usability. Technology had reached the point where only small incremental improvements could be made to game visuals. Then along came the Wii with its revolutionary user-experience approach, which was reflected in a statement made by its then-president, the late Satoru Iwata, at the 2006 Game Developers Conference: "Above all, video games are meant to be just one thing: fun. Fun for everyone."[108]

A year earlier when the Wii was still in development, he gave a strong indication of what Nintendo was trying to do: "We are trying to capture the widest possible audience, all around the world."[109]

The Wii proved to be an instant and enduring hit for Nintendo. In the first year of its release, its half-yearly sales beat the combined total of its two main rivals at the time — Sony's PlayStation 3 and Microsoft's Xbox 360.[110] The Wii's popularity saw Nintendo struggle to keep up with demand in the early years, with stores around the world often quickly selling out of the device.[111]

The Wii console was also a profitable device for Nintendo to manufacture and sell, unlike the PlayStation or Xbox 360 consoles.[112] Both Sony and Microsoft had gone with the approach of taking a loss on their consoles that they would recoup by having high profit margins on their accompanying video games. But Nintendo managed to have their cake and eat it, too. The revolutionary nature of their approach allowed them to make a profit on the sale of both the Wii console and its accompanying games. Company profits soared.

By 2013, the Wii console had achieved 100 million worldwide sales in just over seven years after its launch.[113] Its Wii game sales ran into the billions, with the most popular being its Wii Sports range, which had sold more than eighty million units alone by 2017.[114] A focus on chasing new markets proved to be a resounding success for Nintendo.

Strategies for creating distance from your existing customers

Your loyal customers are what keep you fed as an organization; they're your lifeblood and why you get up in the morning. We love loyal customers and are not advocating for scrapping them. We just think it's worth your while to explore some new customer groups.

Professors Chan Kim and Renée Mauborgne, the authors of *Blue Ocean Strategy*, and tech billionaire Peter Thiel, author of *Zero to One*, along with likely oodles of others, have written about the importance of finding new, untapped markets for your product or start-up. "Where is there a market with lots of prospective customers and low competition," is the question that every forward-thinking leader is asking. We're going to throw our hats in the ring with a few different techniques to answer that question.

Reposition an existing product for a new audience

When Nintendo developed Wii, they found a way to make a gaming system relevant to a completely new audience group. They already had expertise in the technology, and once they identified new market segments (seniors, sports lovers, and home fitness fans), they used their expertise to redesign the traditional game console and create something that the new audiences would love to use.

Are there ways you could redesign your product or service connect with a new, untapped audience group?

Try this brainstorming exercise to challenge yourself to consider completely new audiences:

1. Assemble a group of twelve people and invite them to a sixty-minute brainstorm.
2. Write each of the following audience groups on small pieces of paper, fold them up, and stick them in a hat:
   - Retired senior couples
   - Farm families with young kids
   - Male Gen Zers
   - New immigrants to your country
   - Food bloggers
   - Blue collar workers
   - Fitness instructors
   - Female empowerment groups
   - University professors
   - Interior designers
   - Grade seven students
   - Forty-year-old same-sex couples
   - Advertising creatives
   - Accountants
   - YEMMies (young, educated, millennial moms)
   - Civil servants
   - Sports enthusiasts
   - Small business owners

- Reddit users
- DIY home renovators

3. Break participants into four groups of three people. Get each group to draw an audience from the hat and spend fifteen minutes brainstorming ways you could make your current product relevant to them. Here are a few questions for groups to consider:

  - How can we change our product packaging to get the new audience to buy?
  - How can we change the delivery method to get the new audience to buy?
  - How can we modify our offering so it's relevant and helpful to this audience?
  - How can we change our product features to get the new audience to buy?
  - If version two of this product was tailored exclusively to the new audience, what would it look like?

4. At the end of the fifteen minutes, give each group three minutes to pitch their reinvented product back to the larger group. Document all the ideas.
5. Change up the groups, draw new audiences, and repeat with another fifteen-minute brainstorm and pitch-back session. Document all the ideas.

Find your ten-times-better product

Earlier in this chapter, we talked about the fact that your product needs to be ten times better than the competition's in order to get one of their customers to switch. What does that ten-times-better product look like? More importantly, will that product enable you to attract hordes of new customers without abandoning the existing ones who have taken your company this far?

Try this two-part brainstorming exercise to answer those questions.

1. **Brainstorm your customers' future state**

   Get participants to answer the questions to complete the following matrix:

	A	B	C
	Who are they? (Demographics, psychographics)	What are they doing? (Career, hobbies, family)	Why would a competitor or disruptor target them?
Today			
Five years from now			

2. **Brainstorm customers' needs**

   Get participants to answer the questions to complete the following matrix:

	A	B	C
	What unfulfilled needs do current customers have?	Is there another potential audience group that shares the same unfulfilled need?	How could a competitor or disruptor meet this need?
Today			
Five years from now			

Answering these questions in step one should reveal the type of people your current customers will become and why those people are considered to be valuable to your industry.

In step two, answering the questions in column A should guide future product and service development — they are ways you can enrich the lives of current customers to earn their loyalty.

The answers in column B should reveal another group of people who you could target with your new products or services. Column C is a list of low-hanging fruit. These are the product and services that someone else will certainly begin offering if you don't.

What's next? These matrices are your beginnings of a business case. Pick a few ideas to elevate to your product development team, and see which ones you can implement this year. Then, add the audiences in step two, column B to your marketing plan.

Finding middle ground

While we want to be conscious of what's next for our customers and who we might be able to target in the future, it's hard (and usually not very wise) to abandon existing customers. What we want to do instead is leverage existing customer needs by examining future customer needs. Find specific initiatives that will allow you to access a new market while still remaining relevant for loyal customers.

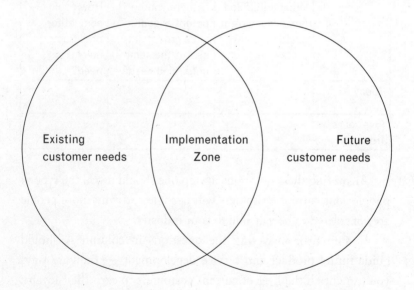

Based on the last couple of exercises, try filling out one of these customer innovation charts. Populate the circles with information on one of your existing customers and a new, radically different customer with whom you'd love to connect. Identify what both groups want, and then implement the service or product feature that both groups desire. It will likely be a stretch, but you'll know the new offering provides value to existing and new customers.

9.

KEEP A HEALTHY DISTANCE FROM PARTNERS

Client intimacy is bad for ideas; keep creative partners in the stranger zone.

"I'm sorry, but I'm letting you go."

"What! Why? We've been together for ten years."

"There's someone new, someone who can make the big changes I want."

"I didn't know you wanted big changes. I can do big changes."

"It's too late, we've already hired a new agency."

Any veteran marketing professional has had this breakup conversation with their agency; the separation is inevitable.

Why do long-term relationships between agencies and clients typically get worse and worse, rather than better and better? It's because two incompatible agency offerings bash up against each other until one wins out, creating a Proximity Paradox. The first offering is creative ideas — novel, out-there advertising concepts and marketing campaigns. The second offering is client intimacy

— the agency's ability to understand the client's business, challenges, opportunities, hopes, and fears.

Creative work is fundamentally *uncomfortable,* because it is new. Client intimacy is fundamentally *comfortable,* because it is familiar. These two opposing offerings are the source of much conflict between both you and your external partners (whether it's an agency or any long-term consultant hired to inject innovation in the company). You both want to push and challenge new ideas, but you both want to find efficiencies in working together. The external partner wants to make a good margin, and you want to work with people who really understand your organization.

In my experience, the comfort of client intimacy eventually trumps the discomfort of creative work.

When client intimacy becomes a bad thing — an ad agency pro's firsthand perspective

Getting closer to the client, establishing great working relationships, collaboration, really understanding your client's challenges and opportunities — these are all ways an agency describes client intimacy. It's usually one of the main goals for an advertising agency and many other service-based industries. In a pitch, it's often one of the first things a client will say they value.

And, while client intimacy is extremely important — crucial to creating the most effective, needle-moving work — I want to address an important caveat that all too often gets forgotten: Stockholm syndrome. I'm not talking about legit Stockholm syndrome (hopefully client kidnapping isn't happening), but rather the threat of identifying too closely with the client or vice versa.

Companies work with advertising agencies because they want someone to push their thinking.

The client has to manage internal budgets, politics, approval systems, and sales figures that can often impede creativity. These are the day-to-day operational realities that can sometimes get in the way. They rely on the agency to get away from some of those internal constraints, to "free think" on the brand.

But as the agency gets closer to the client, it may (to the detriment of the work) start to take on some of those internal restraints. Agency account planners will begin to say things like, "They would never go for that," "The sales team won't like this" or "We just need something quick and dirty."

The agency's deep knowledge of the client and their business forms a set of constraints for the advertising concepts and creative. To stay in the client's good graces and work efficiently, they will narrow the creative spectrum of the ideas they present. It's a great model for quickly producing marketing materials that keep internal stakeholders happy and comfortable, but it's a bad model for uncovering the oddball ideas that might inspire a revolutionary customer engagement campaign or meaningful brand project.

When this happens, the agency essentially becomes the client's internal marketing team. We call this transformation a Proximity Paradox because the people hired for their outsider's perspective inevitably become insiders.

So what am I getting at? Am I saying that we should remove client intimacy from the mix? That we should get further away from our clients to create better, more meaningful work? That client and agency relationships need to change more frequently? Absolutely not.

Client intimacy and a deep understanding of our clients' realities is crucial. The more complex the marketing mix and customer channels, the deeper the understanding required. The more established the agency/client relationship, the deeper this understanding grows. We just need to make sure we actively work to maintain some of that all-important distance.

The curse of legacy clients and longtime agency partners

Walk into any established advertising agency, and you'll find a staple feature: old, boring clients. By old I mean that they're legacy clients — companies that have chosen to work with the same agency partner for more than ten years. And by boring I mean that there are huge constraints on the type of concepts and tactics both the agency and client company will accept.

No one can remember the last time the old, boring client's work was submitted to an awards show or celebrated at a staff meeting. The legacy client's projects are often passed off to agency interns. No one has fun or is excited by the work. It's simply work for the client and the agency.

Old, boring clients are created when there is too much client intimacy. The only way to turn an old, boring client into a fun, exciting client is to introduce a new player on the team — someone with the gumption to shake things up.

I experienced this shake-up firsthand. A new account representative joined the agency and was put on a legacy client's account. She had no prior knowledge of the client, their industry, preferences, or constraints. She looked at the client's marketing goals and budget, and she saw loads of potential. Then she got to work.

She picked some of the bigger-ticket items on the marketing calendar and scheduled blue-sky brainstorms. She brought different agency employees into the brainstorms to inject new energy and ideas. Whenever anyone said, "They'll never go for that," the account rep probed by asking, "Why?" She threw out the old excuses and elevated every idea for which she could make a business case.

The client responded to the fresh ideas and the strategic thinking the new account rep brought to the table. They started saying "yes" to more out-there ideas. Their appetite for risk increased. The agency creative team put new energy into the work, and the agency submitted the client's campaigns to award shows. Within two years, the boring, old client disappeared. A fun, exciting client took its place.

Outsiders can quickly become insiders

As we discussed in the chapters in the first section, people outside your department or leadership team can create the distance your organization needs to break free from the Proximity Paradox. They aren't burdened with the resourcing restrictions, the workloads, the politics, and the counter-creative culture that may exist in your organizations. The right outside help is helpful.

It's for this reason that new agencies and consultants can be so effective in the first few months they work with your organization. It's also the reason that, in the story above, the new account rep was able to transform a boring client into an exciting one.

Consultants have one thing that internal team members do not have: perspective (created by their distance). However, if you lean heavily on these partners for day-to-day support, they'll sink into the same Proximity Paradox problems that you wrestled with yourself. Without some healthy ground rules, your revolutionary outsiders will eventually become complacent insiders.

Without some healthy ground rules, your revolutionary outsiders will eventually become complacent insiders.

Taking an entrepreneurial leap

In recent decades, many established organizations have turned to outside consultants to help them stimulate innovation. Their own organizational resources are often too stretched to effectively do this themselves, or they may want an outside perspective. So, they often pay consultancy firms to identify new opportunities and generate ideas for them via market research.

Depending on the extent of their brief, these innovation consultants may also get involved in helping organizations develop product prototypes and take them through to the commercialization phase. They often also provide advice on the inner workings of the organizations they work with, including restructuring.

One UK-based innovation consultancy that has taken a distinctive approach with the type of consultants and service they provide is OneLeap. This consultancy helps organizations to become more entrepreneurial by providing them with consultants who have been successful entrepreneurs themselves.

However, OneLeap evolved into offering their consultancy service, rather than it being their focus when the company was first founded. They found that there was a significant, unmet demand.

OneLeap began in 2011 as a platform to help aspiring entrepreneurs grow their start-up ventures. It was co-founded by current CEO Hamish Forsyth and advisor/entrepreneur Robyn Scott. Investors, partners and corporate leaders were profiled on OneLeap's website, and budding entrepreneurs could be put in touch with them to pitch their idea for a fee.[115] But OneLeap quickly identified that there was a much greater demand from large, established organizations wanting entrepreneurial advice and support, rather than the other way around (i.e., small start-up ventures wanting support from more established organizations or individuals).

That finding quickly turned their service offering on its head.

OneLeap quickly evolved from being a platform profiling investors, partners, and corporate leaders to one that featured successful entrepreneurs instead. It soon became apparent that this was a unique and valuable consultancy service offering. They now have a network of entrepreneurs spread across thirty-five countries who are available to provide consulting services to large organizations.[116]

OneLeap saw the potential in entrepreneur consultants, rather than the ex-corporate career types that are typically provided by consultancy services.

Large companies often mistakenly think they lack the resources to innovate, but it can be a matter of perspective. Entrepreneurs are used to not having resources and being forced to innovate to do more with less. They usually have firsthand experience doing that to get their own start-up venture off the ground.

Innovation requires focus. Successful entrepreneurs are usually highly focused on their core idea or product/service offering.

Innovation often means going away from the familiar. An entrepreneurial consultant isn't constrained by having to maintain the familiar like an established organization usually is. They will tend to naturally bring this type of experimental thinking into an organization.

OneLeap focuses on assembling unique "one-time" teams of entrepreneurs for any consultancy project. These entrepreneurs are handpicked from their international network on a case-by-case basis, based on the client's requirements and the type of industry they are involved in. OneLeap seeks to match their clients with proven entrepreneurs who have experience that is compatible with their innovation needs.

Forsyth explains the reason why that approach works:

> It works because it's a collaborative process from day one. Another reason is that real entrepreneurs with a proven track record are credible with executives tired of trainers. We only select credible entrepreneurs with a practical mindset into our community.[117]

Their entrepreneurial consultancy teams begin any project by systematically and independently identifying their client company's competitive advantages. This also helps to determine their client's core competencies, which can be a useful starting point for generating potentially suitable innovation ideas.

Each team usually works intensively with a client for about six weeks. During this time, the OneLeap consultants facilitate internal hackathons (known as "venture sprints") at the client organization.

At the beginning of these venture sprints, an innovation challenge facing the organization is clearly defined, along with the parameters for developing an innovative solution. The challenge could be oriented toward a product/service, process, or business model.

Organizational staff at these venture sprints are encouraged to develop and pitch innovative ideas and solutions to their colleagues. For product innovation challenges, they can also build quick prototypes in consultation with OneLeap's entrepreneurial teams. This encourages creative competition and quick decision-making.

The OneLeap consultants carefully select organizational staff to participate in the venture sprints to help ensure maximum impact on the client's organizational culture. Forsyth explains:

> Aside from giving a lot of attention to the personalities and qualities of entrepreneurs we select, we are careful in selecting the participants from the organization as well. We don't just invite the typical innovation champions (CMOs, innovation directors), but also the skeptics.
>
> We also include people from compliance and general counsel. By engaging them in the process and giving them responsibility for making and pitching something, they see things differently. They see themselves differently, and get a sense of creating they did not have before. This helps prevent the corporate immune system from kicking in.[118]

At the end of the venture sprint, the entrepreneurs work with their client organization's management to select the best ideas and/or product prototypes for further development and testing. Those chosen are put through intensive internal and external analysis.

For example, the internal analysis could include investigating the scalability of manufacturing a product innovation. Or it could include determining the feasibility of a service, process, or business model innovation via consultation with all relevant stakeholders.

The external analysis would include the innovation with the organization's existing customers. All this information helps the client organization to get quick and meaningful data about whether or not to proceed with the idea.

OneLeap can return to their client organization after these intensive consultancy bursts to maintain the innovation momentum if necessary. This helps to ensure that innovative ideas don't die a slow death due to the organization losing focus or not devoting the necessary time and resources to see them through to implementation. The consultancy teams can help their organizations to develop and systemize an entrepreneurial approach.

Like other external consultants, OneLeap's teams can also avoid or help to identify any internal politics or structural issues that may hinder the client organization's decision-making and performance.

Perhaps the greatest benefit that OneLeap provides to its clients is access to successful and experienced entrepreneurs who are used to producing fast results when working within limited budgets and time constraints. These entrepreneurs can mimic the environment and enthusiasm of a start-up when facilitating the venture sprint activities with organizational staff.

These entrepreneurs are used to identifying and exploiting opportunities quickly. Speed and spreading the risk are fundamental principles that the consultants try to impart, as Forsyth explains:

Get started on multiple smaller ventures quickly and spread the risk. Your speed has a serious impact on your organizational culture.

It's important to take multiple 'little bets,' because even with the best people, most bets will probably fail — that's the nature of entrepreneurship. If you bet on one grand project and it fails, your entire intra-preneurship strategy will be condemned. I'd rather have teams working on and learning from ten micro-resourced new products or services, than one very well resourced, rigidly defined project venture that has been over-thought.[119]

Essentially, OneLeap aims to create a legacy of successful intra-preneurship within an organization. According to Forsyth:

Successful intrapreneurship is partly about pro-cesses and tools, but mostly about behaviour and culture. You can't change easily. But that change happens by getting people to do, rather than trying to get them to understand new models.

That's why we pair up would-be intrapreneurs and senior executives with proven entrepreneurs to work together to build a prototype venture. Instead of being lectured, it's a hands-on learning experience that delivers ongoing feedback and, crucially, a joint achievement.[120]

OneLeap now works with clients in a broad range of indus-tries, including retail, e-commerce, FMCG, finance, government, energy, travel, and media.

Strategies for creating distance
from your partners

In Part One (Create Distance for People), we shared a number of exercises you can use to create distance with your own internal team. If a vendor or consulting partner is open to shaking things up, we encourage you to try the same exercises with them. Here are a few more strategies you can use to create or restore the healthy distance that should exist between your company and its outside partners.

Mind your "nevers"

Be on the lookout for "client would never" statements. Make a mental note of how often you catch your partner making assumptions about what you would or would not accept. On the flip side, when it comes to your own communication with your outside partner, make a note of how often you say the following statements: "Our team would never go for that" or "I won't be able to get this past my board or management team." These kinds of statements tend to kill an entire creative direction — not just the particular idea up for discussion.

Before shutting down an idea, evaluate it honestly. People can be caught off guard by unexpected recommendations that would require a big change in the team or organization. You may need to check your biases, as we discussed in Chapter Seven. Acknowledge what you like about the idea. Then, ask to set it aside temporarily so you can properly explore its feasibility or merit outside of the meeting. Once you've had a chance to sit with the idea for a few days, circle back with the outside partner to discuss it further.

Be conscious of your hat

In Chapter One, we discussed the Proximity Paradox created by execution ceilings, and we advised you to be conscious of whether you're wearing your innovation hat or execution hat. There are a couple of more names for those hats: outsider's hat and insider's hat.

When you're in a brainstorm with an outside partner, always put on an outsider's hat (a.k.a., the innovation hat). The brainstorm is not the time to talk about internal approvals and creative constraints. Protect the hour of time you have to think freely and push the bounds of your innovation ceiling. Once you've explored as many creative avenues as possible, you can don your insider's (or execution) hat to evaluate the feasibility of the ideas.

In Chapter Three, we shared the brand and vision champion strategy. Bring this exercise into your next meet with your outside partner. Take turns playing the brand champion and the vision champion. Have the partner act as the brand champion, acting practically, and you act as the vision champion, pushing for better ideas and solutions. Talk it out.

Keep the innovation and execution functions separate

One of the primary functions of a consultant is to collaborate with you to solve the challenges facing your team, process, or product. However, an effective consultant takes over the innovation responsibility, so you can focus on the execution responsibility. They should complement — not mirror — what you are doing internally.

For example, the coffee chain Starbucks has an in-house marketing team that handles the execution of all marketing initiatives. They hire an idea agency to generate innovation ideas and strategies. The idea-agency model has gained prevalence in Toronto,

Denver, San Diego, New York and other large cities. The high concentration of marketing and advertising professionals means teams must pick a focus area and recruit outside partners to help with tasks that fall outside that focus area.

Keep the teams fresh

The next time your outside partner schedules a meeting to present ideas or solutions, bring a new colleague to the meeting (someone who has not yet met with the outside partner). Get your outside partner to pitch their ideas to the new face in the room. Get your colleague to provide feedback, ask questions, and analyze the ideas presented. If you can, just sit back and watch — see if you can pick up any limitations either team is placing on the other.

Quarterly "pitch me" sessions

Every quarter, ask your outside partners to pitch you one wild-ass idea just for the sake of pitching the idea. It doesn't need to be well researched or fully fleshed out; it simply needs to challenge the way you currently operate. The more "out there" the better. Make sure you caveat the request by letting your partner know that there is no pressure to produce a workable idea — you just want to see what they are capable of coming up with.

The ultimate goal of this exercise is to kill any assumptions your partner has around your openness to unconventional ideas. Be conscious of how you respond to their ideas. Make sure your outside partner knows the pitch me session is a safe space for creative risk-taking.

It's important to note that these exercises cannot fix all struggling partnerships. You have to be honest with yourself about what your outside partner is producing. Some consultants or agency partners are great at execution and some are great at ideation. It is harder to find a gem who can juggle both responsibilities and do it well. You may be better served by working with a couple of different partners who have perfected their respective processes.

10.

COMPETE WITH THOSE YOU ADMIRE

Want a real advantage over industry competitors? Measure yourself against a different industry.

When Michael Corleone said, "Keep your friends close and your enemies closer" in *The Godfather: Part II*, marketers everywhere took it to heart.

I can't count the number of hours I've spent clustered around an art director's desk, surrounded by my agency teammates, tearing into the new creative released by my client's number-one competitor. It's easy to fixate on a close competitor because gaining a few percentage points in market share, getting more retweets on a social campaign, or winning more awards at a marketing competition all provide a big boost to the marketing or agency teams' egos.

Competitor-monitoring doesn't just happen in the marketing department, either. It can drive the procurement team to adopt a new piece of tech first, or it can spur development to rush a new product to market first.

It's tempting to try and beat your competitor with these small jabs, but if you only try to climb one rung higher on the ladder, you'll often miss the chance to summit a mountain.

In this final chapter, we look at how innovation can be negatively affected when you benchmark against your closest competitor. Often, you need to look beyond your competitors if you want to compete more effectively.

The fierce competition of the equestrian world

I have been a horseback rider for many years, and following college, I began to compete in jumping. The type of jumping I did was called "show hunters." It's a modern-day adaptation of fox-hunting, where well-dressed riders galloped beautiful horses over the English countryside, jumping the fences they encountered along the route.

In the show ring, hunters compete over a course of eight to ten jumps, and a judge scores them on their elegance, rhythm, and style.

To learn how to compete in this sport, I worked with local coaches. They would take me through different exercises designed to improve my skills as a rider and bring out the desirable qualities of my horse. During horse show season, we would attend competitions in my hometown of Winnipeg, Manitoba. I'd ride in my classes and get feedback from my coach, and then we would stand outside the jumping ring and watch other riders compete.

There were a handful of riders who always earned the top placings in the class. I'd study their rides and use them to evaluate my own performance. Year after year, I could not beat them. I was convinced it was because their horses had better jumping style than mine did. In a judged class, style matters. Training can improve a horse's jumping style, but it can't change it entirely. I therefore believed that I couldn't improve my horse enough to beat the top riders.

I didn't realize it at the time, but the Proximity Paradox had led me to believe I could not change my outcomes.

One spring, I had the opportunity to work with a coach who had trained and ridden jumping horses in Florida — a mecca for equestrian sport. Florida was her benchmark, and it was light-years ahead of mine.

In Winnipeg, people compete for six months of the year. In Florida, they travel and compete year-round. In Winnipeg, a non-professional rider can win on a CAD$10,000 horse. But in Florida, a non-pro often needs a US$50,000 horse to win. In Winnipeg, the most prize money paid out at a single competition is CAD$150,000. In Florida, it's US$9 million. You get the picture.

The new coach gave me exercises designed not to help me stay competitive in Winnipeg, but to not embarrass myself according to her Florida-level standards. She broke down every component of my ride, took me back to the basics, and drilled me on perfecting every step of the jumping course — regardless of whether my local competitors were focusing on the same details.

When I entered the show ring again, I had completely different results. My horse still had his flaws, but we had improved every other quality on which we could be judged. Not only did I improve my placings, but I won more prize money that year than I ever had previously (which was, like, $600 — but it felt like a lot more).

What changed? I was riding the same horse in the same city and competing against the same riders. The difference was that the new coach had helped me look beyond my closest competitors, and she benchmarked me against a completely different market. She wasn't blinded by proximity and could see all the areas of my ride that I could improve. She gave me new sources of inspiration and a new standard to shoot for.

Do you have a habit of looking over your shoulder?

According to *Business Insider*, the most competitive jobs in the United States are creative, product, product marketing, IT, finance, procurement engineering, and technology manager.[121] These jobs are high-stakes, have high salaries, and are hard to secure.

According to *Forbes*, the fastest-growing industries in the United States are mining support activities (those that serve oil and gas companies), heavy and civil engineering construction, beverage manufacturing (think microbreweries and taprooms), personal services, and direct-selling establishments.[122] Companies in these sectors are rapidly trying to carve out market share in the race to the top.

If you're in one of those jobs or industries, you'll probably find yourself looking over your shoulder to see who is nipping at your heels.

In highly competitive fields and sectors, it's tempting to focus solely on your competitors. An individual might set up a Google Alert for his competitor's name. A large company might hire a media monitoring company to track its competitor's popularity, influence, and public sentiments.

When the stakes are high, we tend to look over our shoulders to the next competitor in line. We adjust our performance based on theirs; we try to develop a product with a few more features, or we try to populate our resumés with a little more relevant experience.

In business, this "one-up"-driven mindset can lead to two problems:

1. It keeps you focusing on the past (what someone has already produced and put out to the world), rather than your vision for the future.
2. If you're entirely focused on a few key competitors, you won't notice the player at the fringes. And the fringes are where disruptors are born.

You think you're different; they think you're all the same

What's the most boring product you could buy? Some would say it's insurance. Yet what industry wins big at commercial film festivals every year?

Differentiating your insurance company is no small feat. Every provider is selling a similar home, business, and auto product that we begrudgingly pay for once a year and then, in most cases, forget about completely for another twelve months. That's why insurance providers try to differentiate themselves through branding and advertising. They throw big dollars at creating delightful, shareable Super Bowl and prime-time commercials. But let's take a closer look.

If you were to put Progressive's quirky Flo, Allstate's grizzled Mayhem, and GEICO's lizards and raccoons in a room together, you'd see they're not that different. The Proximity Paradox has created a motley crew of spokespeople, all trying to one-up each other in their unexpectedness.

While the spokespeople may feel different to the marketing teams behind them, they don't actually differentiate the insurance provider from the customer's perspective. It's just another wealthy corporation putting a relatable face on the front door.

Finding your source for inspiration

It's easy to answer the question, "How can we solve this challenge in a faster, funnier, or smarter way than our competitor?" It's a lot harder to answer the question, "How can we solve this challenge in a way that makes our customers' lives easier?"

Constraints make brainstorming easier, which is why the first question is easier to answer. It points you in a direction and hints at the picture of success (the solution that is faster, funnier, or smarter than the competition's solution). The second question has no direction and no picture. It's going to take a lot more time and effort to arrive at the aha moment.

In *How to Fly a Horse*, tech investor Kevin Ashton writes, "Creators spend almost all their time creating, persevering despite doubt, failure, ridicule, and rejection until they succeed in making something new and useful." And he goes on to say, "Creating is not magic, but work."[123]

Wouldn't you prefer to invest those hours of doubt, failure, ridicule, and rejection into an idea you really care about, rather than a modification of your competitor's idea? If you do, you must set new benchmarks and find new sources of inspiration — and the best place to look is in a completely different industry.

For example, Louis Pasteur was a chemist with average grades — not a biologist, let alone an expert in invertebrates — when he discovered the cause of silkworm disease and saved the French silk industry in 1870. The Wright brothers were bicycle makers until they built the first successful airplane. History's most celebrated breakthroughs rarely came from someone inside the industry.

If you want to compete, take a page from the playbook of these inventors and learn to look beyond your industry competitors to find your next stroke of genius.

Airbnb — the competitor no one saw coming

You can be sure that no one in the accommodation industry saw Airbnb coming. It's a highly competitive industry where the players constantly compare themselves. But Airbnb managed to disrupt them. And the three founders of the company weren't even working in the accommodation industry. They were all entrepreneurial in spirit, but were also looking to make ends meet at the time.

We've all been in that position at some stage in our lives, but the Airbnb founders thought outside the box when they were in that situation. They came up with an idea to solve a problem that travelers all over the world experience every day: how to find a cheap place to stay. They used contemporary technology to come up with a practical, forward-thinking solution that had never been tried before. It wasn't one that traditional accommodation providers had ever considered because it largely turned their business model on its head.

The Airbnb founders' idea has also helped people earn additional income by temporarily renting out their properties or parts of their properties. It's a win-win-win situation for individuals looking for accommodation, individuals prepared to provide accommodation, and Airbnb.

The competitors that Airbnb disrupted are the traditional accommodation providers who now have yet another major threat to deal with, one that is completely different from any they have ever faced.

In 2007, Brian Chesky and Joe Gebbia were both twenty-seven years old and sharing an apartment in San Francisco. They had gone to college together and studied industrial design, but both harbored ambitions to be entrepreneurs. They worked for about two years after graduation before quitting their jobs to focus on their dream, even though they weren't sure what they were going to do.

As fate would have it, the week they quit their jobs, their landlord raised their rent by twenty percent. But a major global design conference (the Connecting 2007 World Design Congress[124]) was coming to San Francisco the following month, and all the city's hotels had already sold out well in advance.

Being strapped for cash, Chesky and Gebbia thought they could rent space in their apartment to a designer who needed a place to stay. An inflated airbed was the only realistic sleeping option they would be able to offer their guest.

It was a lightbulb moment for them. Other designers in San

Francisco might also like to offer accommodation, too. Maybe it could be their entrepreneurial venture! Below is the transcript of the actual email Gebbia sent to Chesky the next day (complete with its minor punctuation and spelling errors).

> From: Joe Gebbia
> Date: September 26, 2007
> To: Brian Chesky
> Subject: conference
>
> brian
>
> i came up with a name for turning the house into a place to stay...
>   airbed & breakfast
>   ha!
>   airbedandbreakfast.com will be a simple 4 page site or so.
>   then it occurred to me that it could be a place for other designer people in san francisco to list a room (or airbed) in their own houses specifically for the conference. and if we hurry we could ping the idsa to put some of their ubiquitous Connecting '07 ads on it...for a fee, of course.
>   the ideas never end.
>
> joe[125]

The major initial challenge for Airbnb was a variation on the old chicken-and-egg conundrum. To get people willing to advertise their accommodation, they needed to have lots of people visiting their site to see what was available (and to also be prepared to pay for a non-traditional accommodation option). But to get a lot of eyeballs on their site, they needed to have a lot of accommodation listings available in as many areas as possible.

Raising awareness among potential hosts (the sellers of accommodation space) and potential guests (the buyers) of the Airbnb offering was crucial. They needed to establish a critical mass of both groups on their site to be viable.

Renting your home out is not a new concept. But the Airbnb founders put a new twist on an old idea. They saw the opportunity to crowdsource low-cost accommodation for short stays via the web. It relied on the power of the internet to connect strangers and create new opportunities, just like the ride-sharing service Uber successfully did around the same time.

Airbnb has become the trusted intermediary to facilitate the transaction between strangers: the buyer (the guest) and the seller (the host, as the accommodation provider). Similarly, Uber is the trusted go-between, connecting passengers and drivers in its ride-sharing service.

Airbnb further facilitates trust between strangers by allowing both guests and hosts to publicly review each other on its site. They can each provide feedback comments and star ratings on the other. This allows other guests and hosts to evaluate the likelihood that they'll have a good experience dealing with these Airbnb users in the future. Again, Uber uses a similar ratings approach.

Both Airbnb and Uber were fringe players who managed spectacularly and unexpectedly to disrupt very established industries. They focused on solving a problem in a unique way, rather than just trying to solve it using the methods existing accommodation providers were already using. Their solutions were ones that their major established competitors simply couldn't copy.

Gebbia and Chesky created a simple website and emailed some design blogs to promote their new accommodation service. They got three bookings for their own place for the design conference, so they had to buy two more airbeds! It wasn't much, but it was a start and a proof of concept.

A few months later, in early 2008, Harvard graduate Nathan Blecharczyk came on board as a co-founder. He had an IT background and was crucial in setting up Airbnb's online payment and other systems linking hosts and their guests. He also saved an enormous amount of money by renting server space as needed to host Airbnb's website. This wasn't a common practice at the time, but is now standard practice.

For the rest of that year, the Airbnb operation limped along, making some small progress, but nothing to get too excited about. The concept hadn't hit the mainstream consciousness by any means. It wasn't something the average person had ever considered doing.

The company offered three short-term rental types of accommodation:

- Entire homes/apartments (where the guests have the property completely to themselves. The owner can both earn money renting the property and get a house sitter at the same time).
- Private rooms (where the guests get their own room but share the accommodation with others, including potentially the owner of the property, who may simply be renting out a spare room).
- Shared rooms (where guests share a room and the rest of the property with others, including, potentially, the owner. This is the cheapest option, and targets those looking for very cheap accommodation).

The three entrepreneurs tried everything to promote their new business. In January 2009, they even attended the inauguration of President Barack Obama in Washington, D.C. They knew the eyes of the world would be on that historic event, and they wanted to generate some publicity for their fledgling enterprise.

Of course, they used their own service to find a place to stay, arriving a few days prior to the event. They did things like handing out flyers at DuPont Circle metro station in rush hour. The host they chose had rented out his accommodation to others as well. One person had even agreed to stay in the accommodation's walk-in closet!

Chesky thought they could certainly generate some publicity out of that quirky arrangement. He emailed the *Good Morning America* TV program, and one of the producers subsequently included coverage of it in a story about the unusual accommodation options some people had chosen so that they could attend the inauguration.[126]

While that one-off story generated some publicity, it wasn't the ongoing leverage that Airbnb needed. Online ad campaigns became an area of increasingly heavy focus for the company, particularly the use of Google search ads. For example, if someone searched for accommodations in a specific location, Airbnb ads would appear on the top of the search results page.

Airbnb also made extensive use of Facebook's online profiling of its users to target its advertising, which was still a relatively new approach at the time. For example, if a Facebook user's interest was wine, he might receive a targeted Airbnb ad encouraging him to rent a spare room to a wine lover.[127]

Airbnb's highly targeted online advertising approach began to pay dividends. By February 2011, it reached its first significant milestone: one million accommodation nights booked via the site. Less than a year later, that number had quadrupled. It had well and truly reached its critical mass and it has since grown to become the biggest accommodation provider in the world. Even though it owns no hotel rooms, the company is valued at US$30 billion.[128]

In many ways, Airbnb has shared a similar pathway to success as Uber, which similarly hasn't had to invest in any vehicles to shake up the personal transport industry. A focus on a different solution to their potential customers' problems allowed both these start-ups to disrupt established players, without needing a big up-front investment in assets.

It also means that they don't need to tie up their revenue in fixed assets, like accommodation and vehicles, as part of their ongoing operational costs, like the major established players in their industry have done and must continue to do.

And now that Uber and Airbnb are dominant players in their respective industries, neither company has the need to benchmark themselves against their traditional competitors, just like they didn't have that need when they first disrupted them via their innovative business models.

Strategies for creating distance from your competition

Crushing competitors is a natural part of what drives us in business. Competitor successes directly affect our operating budgets and job security. We feel threatened when they do something different, so it's easy to obsess over their activities. That line of thinking is destructive. It can lead us to follow the tracks created by the current market leader. The Proximity Paradox is at work when we begin to question our own actions and miss opportunities to take the business in an alternate (and potentially more lucrative) direction.

To create distance from the competition, set your sights on a new competitor — someone you admire but who operates in a completely different industry. Practice putting yourself in their business's shoes to gain new ideas and an outsider's perspective on your own industry.

Host a cross-industry brainstorm

One of the difficulties in-house marketing teams face is insular thinking. This isn't a result of an inability to think of the big picture, but more a symptom of their proximity to the problems they are trying to solve. In our experience, those old problems are easily conquered when you invite new problem-solvers to the table.

Do you know marketing and creative professionals from a different industry? Try bringing them together to solve business challenges. Professional development organizations are great platforms to meet people and host brainstorming events, so sign up for your local chapter of International Association of Business Communicators, CreativeMornings, The Ace Class, Toastmasters, your alma mater, a or special interest group. Event coordinators for these groups are often looking for new ideas or activities to incorporate into upcoming seminars.

Running a cross-industry brainstorm is easy:

- Ask each participant each to contribute one challenge that they would like others to solve. For context, the challenge should include background info, the audience or stakeholders, objectives, and any important limitations (e.g., budget, geography, timeline, etc.).
- Keep the descriptions short — it shouldn't take longer than thirty seconds to read and understand a challenge.
- Break participants into groups of three to six, then randomly divvy up the challenges among the groups. Have each group pull a challenge from the pile and spend ten to fifteen minutes brainstorming solutions. In an ideal scenario, allow enough time to brainstorm each participant's challenge.
- At the end of the allotted time, have each group stand up and present its solutions to the challenges that it brainstormed.

If hosting an event with a professional development organization is not an option, you can easily gather a few people together and offer to buy them coffee in exchange for an hour of brainstorm power. As the convener of a cross-industry brainstorm, you'll get focused attention on your challenge and dozens of viable ideas. As a participant, you'll get a break from your work routine, discover different brainstorming styles, and may even pick up on some new ideas to try in your own business.

Read another industry's trade publications

Every industry has them: trade publications. You know the ones I'm talking about — the ones that call you every few months asking for ad sales. Love them or hate them, there are a lot of them, and they regularly publish interviews with established and emerging players in the industries they represent.

There is a good chance you've taken a look at what is happening in your industry mags (or, at the very least, you've told your boss that you have done so). But what about looking at another industry's trade pubs? Read the articles and see how these businesses, which have no relation to yours, are innovating:

- What consumer trends are they watching?
- What technology are they adopting?
- What characterizes the new products they are developing?
- How are they changing their delivery model?
- How are they engaging their customers?
- What kind of new departments or skill sets are they adding to their workforce?
- What companies are they partnering with?

There are not always going to be direct transfers, and sometimes you'll have to stretch your imagination, but we promise that you will take away new ideas that you can apply to your business. At the very least, exploring a completely unrelated industry will make you look at your own through a different lens.

Interview a fellow marketer from a different industry

In our own company, we regularly publish "Meet the Marketer" and "Creative Crush" blog posts. We reach out to people we admire, set up an interview and ask them five simple questions. It gives us a chance to network with marketing and creative professionals, and it always inspires some fresh ideas that we can apply to our own business. If you're feeling stuck on a project or at work, try this for yourself.

Hit LinkedIn and search for a marketing professional who works for a company in a completely different industry from your own. If she lives in your hometown, treat her to coffee or lunch. If meeting in person isn't an option, connect for a phone or Skype call. Interview her for a blog post you're going to write that's called, "What I learned about marketing from the X industry" (or something sexier).

Use our list of questions to inspire your own:

- What are some of the biggest opportunities in your industry?
- What are some of the changes happening around you that are freaking you out?
- Describe one project or campaign that you're super proud of, and what you think made it such a success.
- Do you have any guiding principles on marketing?
- You seem to be on the pulse — how do you keep innovating and finding inspiration?

- In marketing, there are often competing forces, including people to please and budgets to keep. Any tips on navigating the creative and practical demands on a marketer?
- What is something you love doing that is completely unrelated to marketing?

Write your blog in a traditional interview format. At the end of the article, include a section of takeaways or learnings. Recap the comments that resonated with you and list a few techniques that you believe you could implement in your own business.

Interviewing marketers regularly is like tapping into a well of fresh thinking that never runs dry. It will energize you and help you examine your company, department, or products with new eyes. You'll discover strategies that have been proven in other industries, and you'll gain the confidence to implement them in your own company. You won't even notice you're crushing the competition next door because you'll be too busy measuring yourself against the marketers and industries you admire.

CONCLUSION

We've been trained to be unoriginal. We are highly attuned to the possibility of risk, and throughout our lives, we've been rewarded for homogeneous thinking. By recognizing our own limitations, we open a whole lot of room for growth. Look to create distance for your people and to create distance from your processes and your industry. This will improve your creativity, innovation, and drive to do things differently.

We wanted to include one more exercise in the conclusion that ties together a few different sections from this book. When you are struggling to break free from your own barriers, your competition, or even your customers or partners, you can try this quick change-the-game exercise. It doesn't need to take long or be too official, but try filling out the table below.

In the "Current state" column, outline your team, processes, competition, audience, and offering in the rows provided. Then, fill out the "Radical change ideas" column and include an out-there or crazy-different idea for how you could change each of the things you outlined in the rows under "Current state." Once you're done, take some time to brainstorm the happy medium between "Current state" and "Radical change." What is one innovation or idea that is easy to implement and points your team or company in a more radical direction? Capture the results of that brainstorm under the column "Incremental change ideas."

Try this exercise every couple of months — you can select one audience or one process to focus on each time. Don't tackle it all at once!

Innovation	Current state	Incremental change ideas	Radical change ideas
Change the team (internal management or project team)			
Change the rules (process, delivery, operation, production)			
Change the competition			
Change the players (audience)			
Change the ball (product, offering)			

Ultimately, we are often our own biggest barriers. Far too often, we get stuck in our own world. We forget to look outside of our situation, our market, or our email account and see the interesting things people are doing all around us. When we do look outside, we can quickly feel defeated and start comparing ourselves to those closest to us. It's human instinct, but it's not doing any of us any favors.

We hope that this book has helped you spot the areas where the Proximity Paradox is impacting your team and your work. We also hope the strategies we shared in each chapter will help you do business in a new way (or at least think about it in a new way).

We encourage you to try even a couple of the exercises in this book. And to remind you to check your proximity. It can pop up where we least expect, and once we are conscious it's incredible to see how many of our decisions it drives.

Happy collaborating, happy distance making and happy innovating! Peace and love, we out. ☺

ENDNOTES

1   Mark J. Perry, "Fortune 500 Firms 1955 v. 2016: Only 12% Remain, Thanks
    to the Creative Destruction That Fuels Economic Prosperity" (2016).
    Accessed on February 13, 2019 through http://www.aei.org/publication/
    fortune-500-firms-1955-v-2016-only-12-remain-thanks-to-the-creative-
    destruction-that-fuels-economic-prosperity/.

2   Sarah Mitroff, "Kodak Sells Digital Camera Patents to Apple, Google,
    Other Tech Giants" (2012). Accessed on December 11, 2018 through
    https://www.wired.com/2012/12/kodak-patents/.

3   Nicholas Taleb, *The Black Swan: The Impact of the Highly Improbable* (New
    York: Random House, 2007).

4   Francesca Gina and Michael I. Norton, "Why Rituals Work" (2013).
    Accessed on December 11, 2018 through https://www.scientificamerican.
    com/article/why-rituals-work/.

5   Anthony P. Carnevale et al, "Recovery: Job Growth and Education
    Requirements Through 2020" (2013). Accessed on December 11, 2018
    through https://cew.georgetown.edu/cew-reports/recovery-job-growth-
    and-education-requirements-through-2020/.

6   Howard H. Stevenson and Mihnea C. Moldoveanu, "The Power of
    Predictability" (1995). Accessed on December 11, 2018 through https://
    hbr.org/1995/07/the-power-of-predictability.

7   "Airbnb Fast Facts." Accessed on December 11, 2018 through https://
     press.airbnb.com/en-uk/fast-facts/.

8   Sean Silcoff, "Winnipeg Startup SkipTheDishes Gobbled up by Britain's
     Just Eat" (2016). Accessed on December 11, 2018 through https://www
     .theglobeandmail.com/technology/winnipeg-startup-skipthedishes-
     purchased-by-britains-just-eat/article33341734/.

9   Trevor Owens and Obie Fernandez, *The Lean Enterprise: How
     Corporations Can Innovate Like Startups* (Hoboken: Wiley, 2014).

10   Jillian D'Onfro, "The Truth About Google's Famous '20% Time'
     Policy" *(2015)*. Accessed on December 11, 2018 through https://www.
     businessinsider.com/google-20-percent-time-policy-2015-4.

11   Adam L. Penenberg, "Dancing Giants: How a Rusting Giant Can Act
     More Like a Startup" (2014). Accessed on December 11, 2018 through
     https://pando.com/2014/03/21/dancing-giants-how-a-rusting-giant-can-
     act-more-like-a-startup/.

12   Jeff Steinberg, "Cultivating Disruptive Innovation in the Enterprise"
     (2016). Accessed on December 11, 2018 through https://www.solutionsiq.
     com/resource/blog-post/cultivating-disruptive-innovation-in-the-
     enterprise/.

13   Marshall McLuhan, "Living in an Acoustic World" (1970). Accessed on
     December 11, 2018 through http://www.marshallmcluhanspeaks.com/
     media/mcluhan_pdf_6_JUkCE00.pdf.

14   Euromonitor, "Breakfast Cereals in Canada" (2016). Accessed on
     December 11, 2018 through https://www.euromonitor.com/breakfast-
     cereals-in-canada/report.

15   Toni Newman, "The 5 Simple Secrets of Innovative Ideas that Get
     Results" (2017). Accessed on December 11, 2018 through https://
     toninewman.com/five-s-solution/.

16   Anne Kingston, "Diamonds Are a Brand's Best Friend" (2008).
     Accessed on December 11, 2018 through https://archive.macleans.ca/
     article/2008/5/19/diamonds-are-a-brands-best-friend.

17   Anne Kingston, "Diamonds Are a Brand's Best Friend" (2008).
     Accessed on December 11, 2018 through https://archive.macleans.ca/
     article/2008/5/19/diamonds-are-a-brands-best-friend.

18   Annette Bourdeau, "Shreddies Don't Want to Be Square Anymore"
     (2008). Accessed on December 11, 2018 through http://strategyonline.
     ca/2008/04/01/creativeshreddies-20080401/.

19   Rory Sutherland, "Life Lessons from an Ad Man" (2009). Accessed

on December 11, 2018 through https://en.tiny.ted.com/talks/rory_
sutherland_life_lessons_from_an_ad_man.

20   Jeromy Llyod, "More Diamonds from Shreddies" (2008). Accessed
on December 11, 2018 through http://marketingmag.ca/brands/more-
diamonds-from-shreddies-17677/.

21   "New Diamond Shreddies" (2008). Accessed on December 11, 2018
through https://cassies.ca/content/caselibrary/winners/2009pdfs/REV_
C08_Shreddies.pdf.

22   Jeromy Lloyd, "Shreddies with a Twist" (2008). Accessed on December
11, 2018 through http://marketingmag.ca/brands/shreddies-with-a-
twist-12890/.

23   "New Diamond Shreddies" (2008). Accessed on December 11, 2018
through https://cassies.ca/content/caselibrary/winners/2009pdfs/REV_
C08_Shreddies.pdf.

24   David Brown, "Diamond Shreddies Wins a Grand Clio" (2008).
Accessed on January 16, 2019 through http://marketingmag.ca/news/
awards/diamond-shreddies-wins-a-grand-clio-15777.

25   "New Diamond Shreddies Wins Grand Prix & Two Golds Cassies 2008
Winners Announced" (2009). Accessed on January 16, 2019 through
https://www.linkedin.com/pulse/five-ss-unexpected-encounters-toni-
newman/.

26   Hunter Somerville, "About/Contact" Accessed on January 16, 2019
through http://cargocollective.com/huntersomerville/ABOUT-
CONTACT.

27   Scott Adams, *How to Fail at Almost Everything and Still Win Big* (New
York: Penguin Group USA, 2013).

28   Mandy Wintink, *Self Science: A Guide to the Mind and your Brain's
Potential* (New York: Barnes and Noble, 2016).

29   "Creating a Responsible and Sustainable Business." Accessed on
January 16, 2019 through http://www.ey.com/us/en/about-us/corporate-
responsibility/corporate-responsibility---our-communities.

30   Emma Hall, "Havas Lofts Program Encourages Global Talent Swap"
(2015). Accessed on January 16, 2019 through http://adage.com/article/
news/havas-lofts-program-encourages-global-talent-swap/298415/.

31   "Future Talent Strategies: How to Keep Employees Engaged" (2014).
Accessed on January 16, 2019 through https://www.slideshare.net/
TalentBites1/future-talent-strategies.

32   Emma Hall, "Havas Lofts Program Encourages Global Talent Swap"

(2015). Accessed on January 16, 2019 through http://adage.com/article/news/havas-lofts-program-encourages-global-talent-swap/298415/.

33   "Havas Lofts June 2017: Meet the Class" (2017). Accessed on January 16, 2019 through https://medium.com/havas-lofts/havas-lofts-june-2017-meet-the-class-f55f9ffa1351.

34   Malika Toure, "New Talent Tips: How Top Agencies Get, Keep and Develop the Best" (2015). Accessed on January 16, 2019 through http://adage.com/article/agency-news/tips-agencies-develop-talent/297476/.

35   "Meet: Patti Clarke, Chief Talent Officer at Havas" (2016). Accessed on January 16, 2019 through http://mag.havas.com/meet-patti-clarke-chief-talent-officer-havas-group/.

36   Yuyu Chen, "Agencies fight turnover, poaching with global job swaps" (2017). Accessed on January 16, 2019 through https://digiday.com/marketing/agencies-develop-talent-swap-programs-give-staffers-global-experience/.

37   Ravi Balakrishnan, "Fast Five with Maxus' Lindsay Pattison" (2017). Accessed on February 13, 2019 through https://brandequity.economictimes.indiatimes.com/news/marketing/fast-5-with-lindsay-pattison/58487570.

38   Saya Weissman, "Agencies Scramble to Keep Young Talent" (2013). Accessed on January 16, 2019 through https://digiday.com/marketing/agencies-keep-talent/.

39   Maureen Morrison, "Want to Retain Agency Staffers? Consider an International Desk Swap" (2014). Accessed on January 16, 2019 through http://adage.com/article/agency-news/swap-desk-program-retains-staff-giving-global-experience/294935/.

40   Ricki Green, "Chris D'Arbon: Jumping in the Deutsche End — Sharing a Creative Exchange in Hamburg" (2017). http://www.campaignbrief.com/2017/08/chris-darbon-jumping-in-the-deutsche-end---sharing-a-creative-exchange-in-hamburg.html.

41   Paul Arden, *It's Not How Good You Are, It's How Good You Want to Be* (London: Phaidon Press, 2003).

42   Giselle Abramovich, "Why Intuit Encourages Job Swaps" (2013). Accessed on January 16, 2019 through https://digiday.com/marketing/why-intuit-encourages-job-swaps/.

43   Francine Katsoudas, "A Great Day at Cisco" (2016). Accessed on January 16, 2019 through https://blogs.cisco.com/news/a-great-day-at-cisco.

44   "Tesco and Coca-Cola Scoop ECR Supply Chain Award" (2013). Accessed on January 16, 2019 through https://supplychainanalysis.igd

.com/retailers/tesco/news/news-article/t/tesco-and-coca-cola-scoop-ecr-supply-chain-award/i/13678.

45   "Coca-Cola Enterprises & Tesco Claim Top ECR Europe Award with 'Job Swap' Collaboration Initiative" (2013). Accessed on February 13, 2019 through http://www.fdbusiness.com/coca%E2%80%91cola-enterprises-tesco-claim-top-ecr-europe-award-with-job-swap-collaboration-initiative/.

46   Mandy Wintink, *Self Science: A Guide to the Mind and Your Brain's Potential* (New York: Barnes and Noble, 2016).

47   Neal J. Roese, "'I Knew It All Along . . . Didn't I?'—Understanding Hindsight Bias" (2012). Accessed on January 16, 2019 through https://www.psychologicalscience.org/news/releases/i-knew-it-all-along-didnt-i-understanding-hindsight-bias.html.

48   Tom Batchelor and Christopher Hooton, "Pepsi advert with Kendall Jenner pulled after huge backlash" (2017). Accessed on January 16, 2019 through https://www.independent.co.uk/arts-entertainment/tv/news/pepsi-advert-pulled-kendall-jenner-protest-video-cancelled-removed-a7668986.html.

49   John Gall, *The Systems Bible: The Beginner's Guide to Systems Large and Small* (Walker: General Symantics Press, 2002).

50   Walter Isaacson, *Steve Jobs* (New York: Simon & Schuster, 2011).

51   Austin Carr, "Apple's Inspiration for the iPod? Bang & Olufsen, Not Braun" (2013). Accessed on January 16, 2019 through https://www.fastcodesign.com/3016910/apples-inspiration-for-the-ipod-bang-olufsen-not-dieter-rams.

52   Doug Aamoth, "Watch Steve Jobs Unveil the iPod 13 Years Ago" (2014). Accessed on January 16, 2019 through http://time.com/3533908/ipod-turns-13/.

53   Philip Michaels, "Timeline: iPodding through the Years" (2006). Accessed on January 16, 2019 through https://www.macworld.com/article/1053499/home-tech/ipodtimeline.html.

54   "iTunes Music Store Downloads Top 25 Million Songs" (2003). Accessed on January 16, 2019 through https://www.apple.com/newsroom/2003/12/15iTunes-Music-Store-Downloads-Top-25-Million-Songs/.

55   James Kerin, "A History of Apple Stock Increases" (2012). Accessed on January 16, 2019 through http://www.investopedia.com/articles/stocks/12/history-apple-stock-increases.asp.

56   Felix Richter, "The Slow Goodbye of Apple's Former Cash Cow"

(2017). Accessed on January 16, 2019 through https://www.statista.com/chart/10469/apple-ipod-sales/.

57   Mic Wright, "The Original iPhone Announcement Annotated: Steve Jobs' Genius Meets Genius" (2015). Accessed on January 16, 2019 through https://thenextweb.com/apple/2015/09/09/genius-annotated-with-genius/.

58   "100 Million iPods Sold" (2007). Accessed on January 16, 2019 through https://www.apple.com/newsroom/2007/04/09100-Million-iPods-Sold/.

59   James Kerin, "A History of Apple Stock Increases" (2012). Accessed on January 16, 2019 through http://www.investopedia.com/articles/stocks/12/history-apple-stock-increases.asp.

60   Eric Jackson, "Apple Music Could Lead to Apple Spending $10 Billion Annually on Content" (2017). Accessed on January 16, 2019 through https://www.cnbc.com/2017/06/12/apple-music-10-billion-a-year-on-content-is-possible.html.

61   John Gall, *The Systems Bible: The Beginner's Guide to Systems Large and Small* (Walker: General Symantics Press, 2002).

62   "Seth Godin's Startup School" (2012). Accessed on February 13, 2019 through http://www.earwolf.com/show/startup-school/.

63   Liz Ryan, "How to Trust Your Intuition and Listen to Your Gut" (2017). Accessed on January 16, 2019 through https://www.forbes.com/sites/lizryan/2017/02/25/how-to-trust-your-intuition-and-listen-to-your-gut/#7ed708f95918.

64   Nick Saint, "If You're Not Embarrassed by the First Version of Your Product, You've Launched Too Late" (2009). Accessed on January 16, 2019 through http://www.businessinsider.com/the-iterate-fast-and-release-often-philosophy-of-entrepreneurship-2009-11.

65   Critics contest whether Darwin actually said this, but regardless of the quote's origin, we feel the sentiment rings true.

66   "Cost of Bringing a Biotech Crop to Market" (2011). Accessed on January 16, 2019 through https://croplife.org/plant-biotechnology/regulatory-2/cost-of-bringing-a-biotech-crop-to-market/.

67   Ken Yarmosh, "How Much Does an App Cost: A Massive Review of Pricing and Other Budget Considerations" (2015). Accessed on January 16, 2019 through https://savvyapps.com/blog/how-much-does-app-cost-massive-review-pricing-budget-considerations.

68   Ken Yarmosh, "How Long Does It Take to Make an App?" (2016). Accessed on January 16, 2019 through https://savvyapps.com/blog/how-long-does-it-take-to-make-an-app.

69   Sienrak, "Ignored by venture capitalists, Pebble Smartwatch Has Raised Over $4M on Kickstarter and Counting" (2012). Accessed on January 16, 2019 through https://venturebeat.com/2012/04/18/pebble-smartwatch-rejected-vcs-kickstarter/.

70   Gillian Shaw, "Vancouver-Born Entrepreneur's Pebble Smartphone Breaks Kickstarter Record" (2012). Accessed on January 16, 2019 http://vancouversun.com/news/staff-blogs/vancouver-born-entrepreneurs-pebble-smartphone-breaks-kickstarter-record.

71   "Pebble: E-Paper Watch for iPhone and Android." Accessed on January 16, 2019 https://www.kickstarter.com/projects/getpebble/pebble-e-paper-watch-for-iphone-and-android.

72   Gillian Shaw, "Vancouver-Born Entrepreneur's Pebble Smartphone Breaks Kickstarter Record" (2012). Accessed on January 16, 2019 http://vancouversun.com/news/staff-blogs/vancouver-born-entrepreneurs-pebble-smartphone-breaks-kickstarter-record.

73   Harish Jonnalagadda, "Pebble Shuts Down Following Fitbit Acquisition" (2016). Accessed on January 18, 2019 through https://www.androidcentral.com/pebble-shuts-down-following-fitbit-acquisition.

74   Dan Seifert, "Pebble Has Now Sold Over 1 Million Smartwatches" (2015). Accessed on January 16, 2019 https://www.theverge.com/2015/2/2/7947799/pebble-1-million-smartwatches-sold-new-hardware-coming.

75   "Pebble 2, Time 2 + All-New Pebble Core." Accessed on January 16, 2019 https://www.kickstarter.com/projects/getpebble/pebble-2-time-2-and-core-an-entirely-new-3g-ultra.

76   "Pebble Time - Awesome Smartwatch, No Compromises." Accessed on January 16, 2019 https://www.kickstarter.com/projects/getpebble/pebble-time-awesome-smartwatch-no-compromises.

77   Lauren Goode, "Fitbit Bought Pebble for Much Less Than Originally Reported" (2017). Accessed on January 16, 2019 https://www.theverge.com/2017/2/22/14703108/fitbit-bought-pebble-for-23-millionw.

78   Steven Levy, "The Inside Story Behind Pebble's Demise" (2016). Accessed on January 16, 2019 https://www.wired.com/2016/12/the-inside-story-behind-pebbles-demise/.

79   Carol Dweck, *Mindset: The New Psychology of Success* (Clitheroe, United Kingdom: Joosr, 2015).

80   Bouree Lam, "The Wasted Workday" (2014). Accessed on January 18, 2019 through https://www.theatlantic.com/business/archive/2014/12/the-wasted-workday/383380/.

81   Steven Bertoni, "Silicon Alley's First Billionaire Aims to Dominate
      Images On Web" (2013). Accessed on Janaury 28, 2019 through https://
      www.forbes.com/sites/stevenbertoni/2013/10/09/silicon-alleys-first-
      billionaire-aims-to-dominate-images-on-web/#5b437be033b2.

82   "The Anatomy of a Hackathon: A 24-Hour Infographic" (2014).
      Accessed on January 18, 2019 through https://www.shutterstock.com/
      blog/hackathon-infographic-shutterstock.

83   Adam Bryant, "Jon Oringer of Shutterstock, on the Power of the
      Hackathon" (2013). Accessed on January 18, 2019 through http://www
      .nytimes.com/2013/06/21/business/jon-oringer-of-shutterstock-on-the-
      power-of-the-hackathon.html.

84   Ritika Trikha, "3 Tips for Dominating Hackathons" (2015). Accessed
      on January 18, 2019 through https://blog.hackerrank.com/3-tips-
      dominating-hackathons/.

85   "Recapping Shutterstock's Annual Hackathon" (2012). Accessed on
      January 18, 2019 through https://www.shutterstock.com/blog/2012/08/
      hackathon-2012/.

86   Anthony Ha, "Inside Shutterstock's Fourth Annual Hackathon" (2015).
      Accessed on January 18, 2019 through https://techcrunch.com/2014/07/22/
      shutterstock-hackathon/.

87   Dan Schwartz, "Inside Offset, Shutterstock's Surreal, Millennial-
      Targeted Stock Image Brand" (2015). Accessed on January 18, 2019
      through https://www.vice.com/en_us/article/yvx8eb/inside-offset-the-
      surreal-millennial-targeted-photo-market-within-shutterstock-111.

88   "Shutterstock Reports Fourth Quarter and Full Year 2016 Financial
      Results" (2017). Accessed on January 18, 2019 through https://www
      .prnewswire.com/news-releases/shutterstock-reports-fourth-quarter-
      and-full-year-2016-financial-results-300413735.html.

89   Joshua Tauberer, "How to Run a Successful Hackathon" (2014). Accessed
      on January 18, 2019 through https://hackathon.guide/.

90   Leo Babauta, "10 Steps to Take Action and Eliminate Bureaucracy"
      (2008). Accessed on January 28, 2019 through https://zenhabits.net/10-
      steps-to-take-action-and-eliminate-bureaucracy/.

91   Josh Bersin, "New Research Shows Why Focus on Teams, Not Just
      Leaders, Is Key to Business Performance" (2016). Accessed on January
      18, 2019 through https://www.forbes.com/sites/joshbersin/2016/03/03/
      why-a-focus-on-teams-not-just-leaders-is-the-secret-to-business-
      performance/#e3651ba24d5a.

92   Dan Goleman, "Retrain Your Stressed-Out Brain" (2011). Accessed on January 18, 2019 through https://www.psychologytoday.com/blog/the-brain-and-emotional-intelligence/201106/retrain-your-stressed-out-brain.

93   Jena Field, "The Science Behind Creativity—What Happens in the Brain and Why" (2016). Accessed on January 18, 2019 through http://openforideas.org/blog/2016/10/12/the-science-behind-creativity-what-happens-in-the-brain-and-why/.

94   Gore Hamel, "Innovation Democracy: W.L. Gore's Original Management Model" (2010). Accessed on January 18, 2019 through http://www.managementexchange.com/story/innovation-democracy-wl-gores-original-management-model.

95   "Nurturing a Vibrant Culture to Drive Innovation" (2008), Accessed on January 18, 2019 through http://techtv.mit.edu/videos/16462-nurturing-a-vibrant-culture-to-drive-innovation.

96   "Case Analysis by Team Bolt" (2017). Accessed on January 18, 2019 through https://www.ukessays.com/essays/business/case-analysis-by-team-bolt-business-essay.php.

97   Paul Hobcraft, "Understanding Innovation the W L Gore Way" (2011). Accessed on January 18, 2019 through http://innovationexcellence.com/blog/2011/09/28/understanding-innovation-the-w-l-gore-way/.

98   "The Gore Story." Accessed on January 18, 2019 through https://www.gore.com/about/the-gore-story#section30031.

99   Alan Deutschman, "The Fabric of Creativity" (2004). Accessed on January 18, 2019 through https://www.fastcompany.com/51733/fabric-creativity.

100   "What It's Like to Lead a Non-Hierarchical Workplace" (2015). Accessed on January 18, 2019 through http://www.wbur.org/hereandnow/2015/07/01/wl-gore-ceo-terri-kelly.

101   "Most Famous Social Network Sites Worldwide as of January 2018, Ranked by Number of Active Users (in Millions)" (2018). Accessed on January 28, 2019 through https://www.statista.com/statistics/272014/global-social-networks-ranked-by-number-of-users/.

102   Kevin Roberts, *Lovemarks.* (New York: PowerHouse, 2007).

103   Nir Eyal, *Hooked: How to Build Habit-Forming Products* (London: Penguin, 2015).

104   John T. Gourville, "Eager Sellers and Stony Buyers: Understanding the Psychology of New-Product Adoption" (2016). Accessed on January 28,

2019 through https://hbr.org/2006/06/eager-sellers-and-stony-buyers-understanding-the-psychology-of-new-product-adoption.

105 "Nikkei Talks with Nintendo's Yamauchi and Iwata" (2006). Accessed on January 28, 2019 through https://web.archive.org/web/20060127211555/http://game-science.com/news/000406.html.

106 "Nintendo Hopes Wii Spells Winner" (2006). Accessed on January 28, 2019 through http://usatoday30.usatoday.com/tech/gaming/2006-08-14-nintendo-qa_x.htm.

107 Edward G. Anderson Jr. and Nitin R. Joglekar, *The Innovation Butterfly: Managing Emergent Opportunities and Risks During Distributed Innovation* (New York: Springer, 2012).

108 Elaine Yu and Wilfred Chan, "8 Memorable Quotes from Nintendo President Satoru Iwata" (2015). Accessed on January 28, 2019 through http://edition.cnn.com/2015/07/13/asia/gallery/japan-satoru-iwata-quotes/index.html.

109 Elaine Yu and Wilfred Chan, "8 Memorable Quotes from Nintendo President Satoru Iwata" (2015). Accessed on January 28, 2019 through http://edition.cnn.com/2015/07/13/asia/gallery/japan-satoru-iwata-quotes/index.html.

110 Ben Kuchera, "Nintendo the Big Winner, PS3 Dead Last for the First Half of 2007" (2007). Accessed on January 28, 2019 through https://web.archive.org/web/20070915005040/http://arstechnica.com/news.ars/post/20070724-first-half-of-console-sales-for-2007-nintendo-the-big-winner-ps3-dead-last.html.

111 "Christmas Morn Without a Wii?" (2007). Accessed on January 28, 2019 through http://money.cnn.com/2007/07/11/news/companies/wii/index.htm.

112 Roger Ehrenberg, "Game Console Wars II: Nintendo Shaves off Profits, Leaving Competition Scruffy" (2007). Accessed on January 28, 2019 through https://seekingalpha.com/article/34357-game-console-wars-ii-nintendo-shaves-off-profits-leaving-competition-scruffy?page=2.

113 Eddie Makuch, "Wii System Sales Cross 100 million Units" (2013). Accessed on January 28, 2019 through https://www.gamespot.com/articles/wii-system-sales-cross-100-million-units/1100-6412271/.

114 "Top Selling Title Sales Units: Wii" (2018). Accessed on January 28, 2019 through https://www.nintendo.co.jp/ir/en/finance/software/wii.html.

115 "From Six-Degrees of Separation to One Leap for Startup Success" (2012). Accessed on January 28, 2019 through https://unreasonable.is/oneleap/.

116   Beth Altringer, "A New Model for Innovation in Big Companies" (2013). Accessed on January 28, 2019 through https://hbr.org/2013/11/a-new-model-for-innovation-in-big-companies.

117   Anis Bedda, "Take the Leap and Start Intrapreneuring — Fast" (2013). Accessed on January 28, 2019 through https://web.archive.org/web/20140929131140/https://www.intrapreneurshipconference.com/take-the-leap-and-start-intrapreneuring-fast/.

118   Anis Bedda, "Take the Leap and Start Intrapreneuring — Fast" (2013). Accessed on January 28, 2019 through https://web.archive.org/web/20140929131140/https://www.intrapreneurshipconference.com/take-the-leap-and-start-intrapreneuring-fast/.

119   Anis Bedda, "Take the Leap and Start Intrapreneuring — Fast" (2013). Accessed on January 28, 2019 through https://web.archive.org/web/20140929131140/https://www.intrapreneurshipconference.com/take-the-leap-and-start-intrapreneuring-fast/.

120   Anis Bedda, "Take the Leap and Start Intrapreneuring — Fast" (2013). Accessed on January 28, 2019 through https://web.archive.org/web/20140929131140/https://www.intrapreneurshipconference.com/take-the-leap-and-start-intrapreneuring-fast/.

121   Rachel Gillett, "15 High-paying Jobs Everyone Wants but Are Nearly Impossible to Get" (2017). Accessed on January 28, 2019 through https://www.businessinsider.com/high-paying-competitive-jobs-2017-7.

122   Mary Ellen Biery and Sageworks Stats, "These 10 Industries Are Growing the Fastest in the U.S" (2018). Accessed on January 28, 2019 through https://www.forbes.com/sites/sageworks/2018/05/13/10-fastest-growing-industries-u-s/.

123   Kevin Ashton, *How to Fly a Horse: The Secret History of Creation, Invention and Discovery* (New York: Doubleday, 2015).

124   Bruce Nussbaum, "Connecting: The Amazing Design Conference in San Francisco" (2007). Accessed on January 28, 2019 through https://www.bloomberg.com/news/articles/2007-10-13/connecting-the-amazing-design-conference-in-san-francisco-dot.

125   Austin Carr, "Starred: The Email that Launched Airbnb" (2011). Accessed on January 28, 2019 through https://www.fastcompany.com/1792024/starred-email-launched-airbnb.

126   Brad Stone, "The $99 Billion Idea" (2017). Accessed on January 28, 2019 through https://www.bloomberg.com/features/2017-uber-airbnb-99-billion-idea/.

127   Brad Stone, *The Upstarts: How Uber, Airbnb, and the Killer Companies of the New Silicon Valley Are Changing the World* (Boston: Little, Brown and Company, 2017).

128   Brad Stone, "The $99 Billion Idea" (2017). Accessed on January 28, 2019 through https://www.bloomberg.com/features/2017-uber-airbnb-99-billion-idea/.

ALEX VARRICCHIO worked with one of the largest advertising agencies on the Canadian Prairies for ten years, and eventually led the creative department as creative director. He has always had an entrepreneurial spirit and pursued his first business venture at the age of four.

KIIRSTEN MAY has always had a passion for storytelling and creative expression. She's channeled that passion into helping brands and individuals influence their communities through well-told stories. Together, they are the co-owners of UpHouse, a marketing agency, and Crainstorm, a crowd-sourced brainstorming web app.